HOLINESS

The Heart God Purifies

HOLINESS
The Heart God Purifies

NANCY LEIGH DEMOSS

MOODY PUBLISHERS
CHICAGO

Library of Congress Cataloging-in-Publication Data

DeMoss, Nancy Leigh.
  Holiness : the heart God purifies / Nancy Leigh DeMoss.
    p. cm. — (Revive our hearts series)
  Includes bibliographical references and index.
  ISBN-13 978-0-8024-1279-9
    1. Holiness—Christianity. 2. Christian life. I. Title. II. Series.

BT767.D412 2004
234'.8—dc22

2004005168

ISBN 0-8024-1279-3
ISBN-13: 978-0-8024-1279-9

Italics in Scripture references indicate author emphasis.

1 3 5 7 9 10 8 6 4 2

Printed in the United States of America

Lord God Almighty,

Holy is thy wisdom, power, mercy, ways, works.
How can I stand before thee
    with my numberless and aggravated offences?
I have often loved darkness,
    observed lying vanities,
    forsaken thy given mercies,
    trampled underfoot thy beloved Son,
    mocked thy providences,
    flattered thee with my lips,
    broken thy covenant.
It is of thy compassion that I am not consumed.
Lead me to repentance, and save me from despair;
Let me come to thee renouncing, condemning,
            loathing myself,
    but hoping in the grace that flows
            even to the chief of sinners.
At the cross may I contemplate the evil of sin,
            and abhor it,
    look on him whom I pierced,
            as one slain for me, and by me. . . .
Thus may my soul rest in thee, O immortal
            and transcendent one,
    revealed as thou art in the Person and work
            of thy Son,
    the Friend of sinners.

> —From *The Valley of Vision: A Collection*
> *of Puritan Prayers and Devotions*

CONTENTS

FOREWORD

Several years ago, my daughter Karina—whose judgment I deeply respect—read Nancy Leigh DeMoss's *Lies Women Believe* and recommended it to me as a great book. Since then I've come to know Nancy as a precious sister. When I've read her books, and spent time with her doing her radio program or talking on the phone, I've been drawn to Jesus.

Readers can rest assured that *Holiness: The Heart God Purifies* comes out of a life that has firsthand experience with the subject matter. The holiness I've seen in Nancy doesn't scream "Look at me—I want you to be impressed with my holiness." It's not the check-off-the-boxes legalism perfected by the Pharisees and paraded by a thousand Christian groups since. It flows from a heart humbly submitted to Christ's lordship. Nancy's holiness is saturated with grace.

"Be holy for I am holy." God is the reason we should be holy. But He's also the empowerment for our holiness. Many of us are convinced we should be more holy, but we've gone about it wrong. To be holy in our strength, and for our glory, is to be distinctly unholy. To be holy in Christ's strength and for His glory . . . that's our calling, and our joy.

Like Jesus, this book is full of grace and truth — challenging yet winsome, convicting yet inviting. True holiness isn't cold and deadening—it's warm and inviting. It's irresistible. Those who think otherwise have never seen it, but only its caricatures. In this book Nancy strips "holiness" of its baggage, so we see it as it is. And, contrary to popular belief, it's something beautiful.

Yes, there is the carry-your-cross demand. But there's also Christ's assurance, "Come to me, all you who are weary and burdened, and I will give you rest. . . . For my yoke is easy and my burden is light" (Matthew 11:28, 30 NIV).

Holiness is the only path to happiness. Every time I've been unholy it has made me unhappy. Every time I've been holy it has made me happy. Holiness sometimes hurts in the short run, but an hour or day or month or year or lifetime from now, holiness *always* brings happiness. Jesus promised it would: "Happy are the pure in heart, for they shall see God."

Nancy says, "No amount of striving or self-effort can make us holy. Only Christ can do that." Gladly, I want to shout, "That's true!"

She says, "Somehow, the evangelical world has managed to redefine sin; we have come to view it as normal, acceptable behavior—something perhaps to be tamed or controlled, but not to be eradicated and put to death. We have sunk to such lows that we can not only sin thoughtlessly, but astonishingly, we can even laugh at sin and be entertained by it."

Sadly, this time, I say, "That's true."

Each day the God in whose presence the seraphim cry "Holy, Holy, Holy," examines every secret corner of our lives. He's the Audience of One. What really matters is whether *He* is pleased with our lives.

May we humbly acknowledge that when it comes to holiness—with all its sacrifices and rewards and pleasures—apart from Christ we can do nothing. But by His grace and empowerment, we really *can* live so that we may one day hear Him say those amazing, thrilling words: "Well done, my good and faithful servant!"

The moment we hear those words, from the mouth of our Lion and Lamb, we'll know that in comparison, nothing else matters.

RANDY ALCORN

ACKNOWLEDGMENTS

This book has been far from a solo under-taking. Many dear friends and colleagues have labored with me through a lengthy birthing process. I owe special gratitude to:

* The Moody Publishers team—particularly *Greg Thornton, Bill Thrasher,* and *Elsa Mazon* —apart from whose vision, partnership, and perseverance there would not have been a *Revive Our Hearts* trilogy.

* *Dr. Bruce Ware* for your theological review and *Bob Lepine* for your iron-sharpening input and insights throughout the process. Your biblical oversight and "guardianship" of this message have meant so much!

❋ *Del Fehsenfeld III, Steve and Carter Rhoads, Lela Gilbert, Mary Ann Lepine, Elisabeth DeMoss, Betsey Newenhuyse,* and *Josef Tson,* among others, who interacted with me about this vast, grand subject, supplied helpful resources, read the manuscript in part or in whole at various stages, and offered valuable suggestions.

❋ *Dawn Wilson* for your research assistance, *Cheryl Dunlop* for your careful copyediting, and Carolyn McCulley for your creative input on the discussion guide.

❋ *Mike Neises* for countless hours of invaluable behind-the-scenes administrative efforts— you are truly a faithful servant of Christ.

❋ The entire *Revive Our Hearts* team that has so graciously and effectively carried on with the ministry through my extended periods of hibernation, all the while praying and cheering me on—you are an extraordinary group, and I am honored and humbled to be your fellow "under-rower."

❋ I don't know that I have ever had—or needed —more earnest prayer support than that which has undergirded this project from start to finish. Many precious *Praying Friends* have paid a price to see this book born. May God reward your labors, and may He soon grant the revival of holiness for which our hearts long.

INTRODUCTION

Oh for holiness!
Oh for more of God in my soul!
Oh this pleasing pain!
It makes my soul press after God.

DAVID BRAINERD[1]

Nothing could have prepared me for the call I received early one morning about a year ago. A brokenhearted pastor was calling to ask me to pray and to be prepared to reach out to a mutual friend whose husband was about to confess to her that he had been committing adultery with a young woman in their church for the past six months.

I gasped in disbelief. This couple has been among my dearest friends for most of my adult life. From all appearances, they both had a deep, genuine love for the Lord, as well as an unusually strong marriage and family.

Now, this husband had flagrantly broken his covenant with his God and his wife; worse, his heart had become hard and cold. This man who had often been known to weep over his sin was now dry-eyed and unrepentant.

I don't believe it was a coincidence that this call came just as I was getting ready to start writing this book. Or that in the prior three weeks I had learned of several other believers whose "private" sin had become public and created no small eruption.

My passion for the message of holiness has been fueled by these and far too many other real-life stories I have heard and witnessed in the course of working on this book.

The burden on my heart has intensified as I have received letters and e-mails from people who are troubled about what they see going on around them in the church. The following excerpt represents the concern of this remnant of believers:

> The leadership in our church doesn't seem to have the same fire for purity that we want to have. They don't share our sense of right-from-wrong when it comes to things like movie/TV watching, modest dress, and drinking. They seem to think the best way to witness to the lost is to be like them.
>
> My own accountability partner does not have a problem with watching R-rated movies or TV shows that promote fornication, adultery, and blatant sin. Our youth pastor has told me that watching R-rated movies is all right since that's how he keeps in touch

with what the youth of today are exposed to.

We don't want to be divisive or to come across as self-righteous or "legalistic." It's just that the more we learn about purity and godliness, the more we see the dilution of the Christian life around us, and we're at a loss to know what to do about it. My wife and I have wasted too much time "playing church," and we don't want our kids to think that God is a God of compromise. *We're not wrong . . . are we??*

Are they wrong? Are they unnecessarily uptight or narrow-minded? Do these issues really matter? Or are they simply a matter of personal conscience? Do they change with the culture? These are questions I've wrestled with and tried to examine in the light of Scripture.

HOLINESS AND SIN BOTH MATTER—MORE THAN WE CAN IMAGINE.

Something else has haunted me as I've worked on this book. It's the matter of my own heart.

Early in the year-long process of birthing this book, I began to pray this prayer:

> *Oh, God,*
> *show me more of Your holiness.*
> *Show me more of my sinfulness.*
> *Help me to hate sin and to love righteousness as You do.*

*Grant me a deeper conviction of sin
and a more thorough spirit of repentance.
And make me holy as You are holy.*

The result is that as I have worked on this book, the Spirit of God has worked on me. As I have grieved over the subtle (and not-so-subtle) ravages of sin among professing believers and the extent to which the church has adopted the world's values, I've had to face the fact that I am often more bothered by others' failures than by my own shortcomings. I tend to minimize or rationalize in my life certain offenses that disturb me when I see them in others.

As I have wrestled with how to communicate the message of holiness, God has gently and graciously exposed unholiness in my own heart—things like lack of self-control in relation to my tongue, my reactions, and my eating and spending habits. I've had to admit that I love myself more than I love others, that I care too much about the impression I make on others and too little about pleasing God, and that I have set up idols (substitutes for God) in my heart.

As I have pondered both what I've heard and seen in others over these months, as well as my own battle with indwelling sin, the message that has reverberated in my heart is that *holiness and sin both matter*—more than we can imagine. They matter to

God, and the more we comprehend their true nature, the more they will matter to us.

The message of repentance and holiness needs to be proclaimed, heard, and heeded among God's people in every generation. It must become more than a theological tenet that we politely nod agreement to; it needs to transform the way we think and the way we live.

My goal in writing this book is not to offer a theological treatise on holiness.[2] Rather, my heart is to issue an earnest appeal to God's people—those He calls *saints* or *holy ones*—to pursue holiness.

Believe me when I say that I feel even more unqualified to write a book on holiness now than when I began a year ago (unless being a sinner desperately in need of God's mercy qualifies someone to address this subject). But through this process, my heart has become more tender and my conscience more sensitive; I have been given a clearer vision of Calvary and of the incredible, sanctifying grace of God. I echo the words of the hymn writer:

From my smitten heart with tears two wonders I confess:
The wonders of redeeming love and my unworthiness.[3]

I invite you to join me in a pursuit of radical holiness. You can start right now. Before reading on, would you turn back to that prayer on pages 19–20 and make it your own? One phrase at a time, express to the Lord your desire to have a pure heart.

Then I want to encourage you to pray this prayer at least once a day for the next thirty days. As you make these requests to the Lord from your heart, expect Him to hear and to answer!

True holiness is the pathway to fullness of life and joy. To be holy is to be wholly satisfied with Christ. Above all, it is to reflect the beauty and the splendor of our holy Lord in this dark world. In pursuing holiness, you will fulfill and experience all that God had in mind when He created you.

> *Now may the God of peace himself sanctify you com-*
> *pletely, and may your whole spirit and soul and body*
> *be kept blameless at the coming of our Lord Jesus Christ.*
> *He who calls you is faithful; he will surely do it.*
> —1 Thessalonians 5:23–24

NOTES

1. *The Life of David Brainerd,* ed. Norman Pettit, *The Works of Jonathan Edwards,* vol. 7 (New Haven, Conn.: Yale Univ. Press, 1985), 186.
2. Many excellent books on holiness have already been written. Those I have found most helpful include: Jerry Bridges' *The Pursuit of Holiness* (NavPress, 1996), J. I. Packer's *Rediscovering Holiness* (Vine Books, 2000), R. C. Sproul's *The Holiness of God* (Tyndale, 2000), and J. C. Ryle's *Holiness* (Evangelical Press, 1985). I urge you to read these and other such books as part of your personal pursuit of holiness.
3. "Beneath the Cross of Jesus," Elizabeth Clephane, 1872.

THE SPLENDOR
OF HOLINESS

How little people know who
think that holiness is dull.
When one meets the
real thing . . . it is irresistible.

*

*

Holiness isn't exactly an easy subject to "sell." It's not one of the top ten topics people look for in a Christian bookstore; there aren't a lot of hit songs about holiness; and I can count on two hands the number of messages I recall hearing on the theme.

"Holiness" is discussed in theology classes, but rarely in dinner table conversations. "Holy" is an adjective we apply to "Bible," "Communion," and "the night Christ was born." But how many contemporary Christians are really interested in devoting serious thought or discussion to holiness?

We don't mind talking about holiness as an abstract concept. But if that concept gets too personal or starts to interfere with our lifestyle, we can quickly become uncomfortable.

Part of the problem may be that the word *holiness* has picked up some baggage that most people —understandably—don't find particularly desirable. Does "holiness" conjure up any of these images in your mind?

* Somber, straitlaced people with outdated hair and clothing styles

* An austere, joyless lifestyle based on a long list of rules and regulations

* A monklike existence—"holy" people talk in hushed tones, spend hours a day in prayer, always have their nose in the Bible or a spiritual book, fast frequently, hum hymns under their breath, and have no interest in "normal" life activities

* People with a judgmental attitude toward those who don't accept their standards

* An unattainable ideal that has more to do with the sweet by-and-by than the real world, which is right here, right now

Holiness. When you put it that way . . . who wants it?! Sounds about as appealing as drinking saltwater.

Holiness may not be at the top of our list of things to talk about, but let me remind you that those in heaven never stop talking about it! I believe we need to "reclaim" true holiness—to see it in all its beauty, as it is revealed in the Word of God.

I was blessed to grow up in a home where holiness was emphasized and taken seriously, while being presented as something wonderfully desirable and attractive. From earliest childhood, I remember thinking that holiness and joy were inseparably bound to each other.

> "HOLINESS" IS DISCUSSED IN THEOLOGY CLASSES, BUT RARELY IN DINNER TABLE CONVERSATIONS.

My dad longed to be "as pure as the driven snow" and challenged us to aspire to the same standard. He was deeply disturbed by sin—whether his own, ours, or others'. At the same time, my dad was a happy man; he actually *enjoyed* his life in Christ.

Prior to his conversion in his mid-twenties, he had been a freewheeling gambler in mad pursuit of happiness and thrills. When God reached down and redeemed him, his lifestyle changed dramatically— he no longer desired the earthly "treasures" with which he had been trying to fill the empty places of his heart. Now he had found "the pearl of great price" he had been lacking for so many years. He loved God's law and never considered holiness burdensome —he knew that *sin* was the real burden, and he never got over the wonder that God had mercifully relieved him of that burden through Christ.

The eighteenth-century theologian Jonathan Edwards was compelled by a similar vision of holiness. In his memoirs, written at the age of thirty-five, he spoke of the fascination and attractiveness that thoughts of holiness held for him.

It appeared to me, that there was nothing in it but what was ravishingly lovely; the highest beauty and amiableness—a *divine* beauty; far purer than any thing here upon earth; and that every thing else was like mire and defilement in comparison of it.[2]

Likewise, A. W. Tozer saw the need to challenge the misconceptions often associated with holiness.

What does this word *holiness* really mean? Is it a negative kind of piety from which so many people have shied away?

No, of course not! Holiness in the Bible means moral wholeness—a positive quality which actually includes kindness, mercy, purity, moral blamelessness and godliness. It is always to be thought of in a positive, white intensity of degree.[3]

The beauty of holiness, as it shines forth in the Scripture, is seen in two related but distinct facets.

SET APART

The word *holy* comes from a root that means "to cut, to separate." It means "to be set apart, to be distinct, to be different."

Throughout the Scripture, we find that God set apart certain things and places and people for Himself; they were consecrated for His use. They were not to be used for common, ordinary, everyday purposes; they were *holy*. For example,

> THE BIBLICAL
> CONCEPT
> OF HOLINESS
> CARRIES WITH IT
> A SENSE OF
> BELONGING
> TO GOD.

❖ God set apart one day out of the week and called it "a *holy Sabbath* to the Lord" (Exodus 16:23).

❖ The Israelites were required to set apart the first portion of their income as a *holy tithe* (Leviticus 27:30).

❖ God set apart a particular room where He would meet with His people; He called it "the *holy place*" (Exodus 26:33).

In the Old Testament, the nation of Israel was set apart by God to be a "holy nation" (Exodus 19:6). That didn't mean their *conduct* was holy or that they were inherently more upright than others who were not set apart. God called them "holy" because He had set them apart from other nations, and with that distinction and privilege came the obligation to live holy lives.

Not only were the Israelites set apart *by* God— they were also set apart *for* God. "I the Lord am holy and have separated you from the peoples, *that you should be mine,*" God told His people (Leviticus 20:26). The biblical concept of holiness carries with it a sense of belonging to God, much as a mother might claim, "These children are *mine.*"

In the New Testament, God set apart a new body comprised of both Jews and Gentiles. He called it the *church.* The Greek term *ekklesia* means "a called-out assembly." The church is not a building or merely an institution; it is a body of believers who have been called out of this world and set apart for God's holy purposes.

I remember first discovering as a child something of what it meant to be "set apart" for and by God. Based on their understanding of the heart and ways of God, my parents established what they felt to be wise practices and limitations for our family. At times, we would complain, *"But everybody else . . . !"* My parents' response was along these lines: "You don't belong to 'everybody else'—you belong to God!" They convinced us there was something really special about being set apart for God rather than being squeezed into the world's mold.

I learned early on that to be "set apart" is not a punishment; it is not an attempt on God's part to deprive us or to condemn us to a cheerless, joyless lifestyle. It is a priceless privilege—it is a call

> GOD IS HOLY, AND HOLINESS IS NOT AN OPTION FOR THOSE WHO BELONG TO HIM.

* to belong, to be cherished, to enter into an intimate love relationship with God Himself, much as a groom declares his intent to set his bride apart from all other women to be his beloved wife

* to fit into the grand, eternal plan of our redeeming God for this universe

* to experience the exquisite joys and purposes for which we were created

* to be freed from all that destroys our true happiness

MORALLY CLEAN

The second facet of holiness has to do with being pure, clean, free from sin. In this sense, to be holy is to reflect the moral character of a holy God.

If you've ever tried to wade through the book of Leviticus, you may have found yourself wondering, *Why did God bother to give all those detailed instructions about cleansing and ceremonial purity?*

God intended those regulations to be an object lesson to the children of Israel—and to us. He wants us to understand that He is holy, and that holiness is not an option for those who belong to Him. He wants us to know that He is concerned with every detail and dimension of our lives. He wants us to understand the blessings of holiness and the consequences of unholy living.

When we come to the New Testament, we find that God's standard has not changed. Over and over again, Jesus and the New Testament authors call us to a life of absolute purity:

"You therefore must be perfect, as your heavenly Father is perfect." (Matthew 5:48).

Keep yourself pure. (1 Timothy 5:22)

Awake to righteousness, and do not sin. (1 Corinthians 15:34 NKJV)

Let everyone who names the name of the Lord depart from iniquity. (2 Timothy 2:19)

Abhor what is evil; hold fast to what is good. (Romans 12:9)

Holiness is not just for some select few spiritual giants; it is not just for pious people who sit around all day with nothing to do but "be holy."

Holiness is for moms who battle a sense of uselessness and discouragement and who are tempted to escape into self-pity, romance novels, or the arms of an attentive man. It is for students who are constantly bombarded with pressure to conform to the world and to indulge in ungodly forms of entertainment. It is for lonely widows, divorceés, and singles who are struggling to stay sexually abstinent. It is for husbands and wives who wrestle with bitterness toward mates who have abused or abandoned them. It is for men who are tempted to cheat on their expense reports or their wives or to abdicate their spiritual leadership in the home.

> GRACE GIVES US THE *DESIRE* AND THE *POWER* TO BE HOLY.

"*Everyone* who names the name of the Lord" is called to live a holy life!

We're going to explore *how* we can be holy, but it's important to realize that God would not command us to do anything without also enabling us to do it. He knows we cannot possibly be holy apart from Him. That's why He has made provision for us to overcome sin through the cross of Christ. That's why He has sent His Spirit to live in our hearts. And that's why He has given every believer a supernatural resource called *grace* that gives us the *desire* and the *power* to be holy.

The Fruit of Relationship

True holiness is cultivated in the context of a relationship with God. His love for us moves us to reject all lesser loves and all the fleeting delights sin can offer.

As our love for Him grows, we are motivated to aspire to holiness. The fact that He is our Father and we are His beloved children makes us long to be close to Him and compels us to avoid anything that could cause a breach in the relationship.

Yes, holiness involves adherence to a standard, but the obedience God asks of us is not cold, rigid, and dutiful. It is a warm, joyous, loving response to the God who loves us and created us to enjoy intimate fellowship with Him. It is the overflow of a heart that is deeply grateful to have been redeemed by God from sin. It is not something we manufacture by sheer grit, determination, and willpower. It is motivated and enabled by the Holy Spirit who lives within us to make us holy.

EXTREME HOLINESS

The congregation of the Gustaf Adolph Evangelical Lutheran Church, located in a small town in northern Maine, learned just how dangerous a little bit of impurity can be. On Sunday, April 27, 2003, the church council gathered after services to discuss the installation of a new heater. Several in the group stopped by the kitchen to grab a cup of coffee on the way into the meeting. Within hours more than a dozen people were gravely ill, and within days one man had died.

Investigators discovered that a man with a vendetta had dropped a handful of powdered arsenic in the church's coffee urn. No one had noticed the small amount of poison—until its consequences became apparent. Like the bit of leaven that leavens a whole lump of dough, tolerating "just a little sin" in our lives can be deadly.

The makers of Ivory soap pride themselves on their product being "$99\frac{44}{100}$% pure." When it comes to holiness, however, if it's only $99\frac{44}{100}$% pure, it's not pure.

A commitment to be holy is a commitment to be clean through and through—to have no unholy part. True holiness starts on the inside—with our thoughts, attitudes, values, and motives—those innermost parts of our hearts that only God can see. It also affects our outward and visible behavior: "Be holy in *all your conduct*" (1 Peter 1:15).

This passion for purity is what I saw in my dad's example that made holiness so compelling to me as a young person. Of course, he often failed (and was willing to admit it when he did); but he sought to live a life that was morally upright and completely above reproach: in the way he ran his business, used his time, conducted himself with members of the opposite sex, treated family members and employees, talked about other people, responded to his critics, spent his money, and honored the Lord's Day; in his work habits, leisure activities, and entertainment choices—what he read and listened to and watched. He so loved God that he wanted holiness to characterize every area of his life.

He believed, as did Helen Roseveare, a missionary surgeon in (then) Congo, that "there must be nothing, absolutely nothing, in my daily conduct that, copied by another, could lead that one into unholiness."[4]

I have a friend whose ninety- and ninety-two-year-old parents recently moved out of the house where they had lived for fifty years. My friend spent an entire month sorting through a lifetime of their accumulated "stuff"—correspondence, financial data, clippings, photos, and on and on. "It was a complete record of their lives," my friend reflected.

After poring through the massive collection of memorabilia and paperwork, this son observed with a sense of wonder, *"There was not one single thing in my parents' belongings that was inconsistent with their profession of their relationship with Christ!"*

How would you fare if someone were to go through the record of your life—all your possessions, the books and magazines you've read, your CD and DVD collections, checkbooks, tax returns, journals, daily planners, phone bills, correspondence, past e-mails, a record of all your Internet activity?

> HOW WOULD YOU FARE IF SOMEONE WERE TO GO THROUGH THE RECORD OF YOUR LIFE?

What if the person could also review a photographic replay of the choices you've made when you thought no one was watching? Add to that a script of your thought life . . . your attitudes . . . your secret motives.

Does the thought of such "extreme holiness" seem burdensome to you? If so, you may never have considered that *holiness* and *joy* are inseparable companions.

THE JOY OF HOLINESS

What words do you associate with "holiness"? Would *gladness* be one of those words?

Think about it the other way around. When you think of things that make you *glad,* do you think of *holiness?*

> HOLINESS AND JOY ARE INSEPARABLE COMPANIONS.

Surprising as it may seem, *holiness* and *gladness* really do go hand in hand.

In both the Old and New Testaments we find a wonderful description of the Lord Jesus that makes this connection:

> *You have loved righteousness and hated wickedness;*
> *therefore God, your God, has anointed you with the oil of*
> *gladness beyond your companions.*
>
> —Hebrews 1:9; see Psalm 45:7

We might picture someone who has a passionate love for holiness and an intense hatred for sin as being joyless, uptight, and rigid.

In fact, nothing could be further from the truth. The result of Jesus' holy life was overflowing gladness —gladness surpassing that of anyone else around Him. It was true of Jesus. And it will be true of anyone who, like Jesus, loves righteousness and hates evil.

I remember the first time I heard Calvin Hunt share his story. For years, this young man lived an irresponsible, destructive lifestyle as a crack cocaine addict. Then he encountered the irresistible, transforming grace of Christ. To this day, Calvin exudes irrepressible joy as he testifies of the purifying work of God in his life and then lifts up his powerful tenor voice and sings what has become his trademark song, *"I'm clean! I'm clean! I'm clean!"*

Why do we make holiness out to be some austere obligation or burden to be borne, when the fact is that to be holy is to be clean, to be free from the weight and the burden of sin? Why would we cling to our sin any more than a leper would refuse to part with his oozing sores, given the opportunity to be cleansed of his leprosy?

To pursue holiness is to move toward joy—joy infinitely greater than any earthly delights can offer.

To resist holiness or to be half-hearted about its pursuit is to forfeit true joy and to settle for something less than that God-intoxication for which we were created.

> TO BE HOLY IS TO BE CLEAN, TO BE FREE FROM THE WEIGHT AND THE BURDEN OF SIN.

Sooner or later, sin will strip and rob you of everything that is truly beautiful and desirable. If you are a child of God, you were redeemed to enjoy the sweet fruit of holiness—to walk in oneness with your heavenly Father, to relish His presence, to rejoice in His mercy, to know the joy of having clean hands, a pure heart, and a clear conscience, and, one day, to stand before Him unashamed.

Why settle for anything less?

NOTES

1. C. S. Lewis, *Letters to an American Lady,* ed. Clyde S. Kilby (Grand Rapids: Eerdmans, 1967), 19.
2. *Memoirs of Jonathan Edwards,* Works of Jonathan Edwards, vol. 1 (Edinburgh: Banner of Truth Trust, rept. 1974), xiv.
3. A. W. Tozer, *I Call It Heresy* (Harrisburg, Pa.: Christian Publications, 1974), 63.
4. Helen Roseveare, *Living Holiness* (Minneapolis: Bethany House, 1986), 173.

THE MOTIVATION FOR HOLINESS

The serene beauty of a holy life
is the most powerful influence
in the world
next to the power of God.

❊

—BLAISE PASCAL[1]

❊

In spite of all that I know and believe about the "splendor of holiness," there are moments when I think, *It's so hard to have to "be holy" all the time! Why can't I just relax and take it easy sometimes?*

Yes, I understand that holiness isn't about sheer human effort and self-striving. I know it's about depending on God's enabling grace and letting Jesus live His holy life in and through us.

But be honest—don't you find that it often seems a lot easier to go with the flow of your natural, fleshly desires than to deny your flesh and choose the pathway of holiness?

So why swim upstream against the current of your flesh and the culture? Why pay the price to be intentional and vigilant in pursuing holiness—every moment of every day for the rest of your life? Why make the tough, daily choices that holiness requires:

✷ To get out of bed in the morning and wash your heart in the water of God's Word before you jump into your "to do" list?

✷ To turn off that suggestive or crude TV program or to put down that magazine that promotes selfish, worldly values, or that novel that glamorizes sensuality?

✷ To admit you have sinned and seek forgiveness for speaking roughly to that family member or lying to your boss or being critical of that fellow church member?

✷ To say no to every hint of sexual impurity?

✷ To eat and sleep and dress and go to work and play and give and pray and go to church—all for the glory of God?

In this chapter I want to explore seven powerful biblical motivations for holy living—incentives that have been helpful in my personal pursuit of holiness. Above all other reasons, we are to be holy . . .

BECAUSE GOD IS HOLY

As a photograph is an image of an object, so our lives are intended to portray the image of God. People are supposed to be able to look at Christians and see what God is like!

My house sits on a hill overlooking a river. This morning, as the sun shone brightly on the trees across the river, the likeness of those trees with their gorgeous fall foliage was magnificently reflected on the still waters below. The mirror image caused me to pause and pray, "Lord, may others see Your likeness reflected in me; may my life reveal to the world how lovely and pure You are!"

This is the motivation for holiness that is stated in the Scripture more frequently and explicitly than any other reason:

> *But as he who called you is holy,*
> *you also be holy in all your conduct,*
> *since it is written, "You shall be holy, for I am holy."*
> —1 Peter 1:15–16

In our everyday life and conduct, we are to reflect what God is like and what it means to belong to Him and to be His redeemed, "set apart" people. Our lives are to *make God believable* to our world. As they see His image in us, they will be moved to worship and glorify Him (Matthew 5:16).

What does your life reflect to those around you? Do your attitudes, words, and behavior give others an accurate picture of God? Or do you sometimes profane His holiness—perhaps by a complaining or controlling spirit, by harsh or angry words, by participating in coarse conversation, or laughing at off-color humor? It saddens me to think of how often I have given others a distorted perception of God through my ungodlike choices and responses.

> HE IS THE STANDARD FOR YOUR HOLINESS, AND HE IS THE *SOURCE* OF YOUR HOLINESS.

Because God is holy, we must be holy. And here's the good news—because God is holy, we *can* be holy. If you are a child of God, the Holy God lives in you. He is the standard for your holiness, and He is the *source* of your holiness—*He* is your righteousness. He can wash your unholy heart with the blood of Jesus and make you clean—so the world will know what He is like.

To be holy as He is holy—what an awesome responsibility. But more than that, what an astounding privilege—that the Holy One should choose us, earthbound, frail, and flawed as we are, that He should cleanse us from our sins, fill us with His

Holy Spirit, and then use us to reflect the splendor
of His holiness in this dark world.

Here's another motivation to pursue holiness:

BECAUSE HOLINESS IS GOD'S
STATED GOAL FOR EVERY BELIEVER

God's goal in saving you was not just to make
your few years on planet Earth easier or more enjoy-
able. He had an eternal end in
view. His intent was to make you
holy, as He is holy, that you might
perfectly glorify Him, that you
might bring Him pleasure, and
that you might enjoy intimate fellowship with Him for all eternity.

> YOUR HOLINESS
> IS GOD'S
> SUPREME
> PURPOSE FOR
> YOUR LIFE.

The apostle Paul reminds us
that God "chose us in [Christ] before the foundation
of the world, that we should be holy and blameless
before Him" (Ephesians 1:4).

Your holiness is not secondary to whatever other
goals you may have for your life—it is God's
supreme purpose for your life. It is something He
desired, planned, and made provision for before He
even created the world.

Not only is it our individual calling to be holy but
also it is our collective calling, as the body of Christ.
The church is a living organism, indwelt by the Holy

Spirit of God and being prepared to be a bride for the Lord Jesus. And the stated intent of our Bridegroom for His bride is that "he might present the church to himself in splendor, without spot or wrinkle or any such thing, that she might be holy and without blemish" (Ephesians 5:27).

As an earthly groom eagerly anticipates the moment when his bride walks down the aisle to meet him, beautifully arrayed in a spotless, white wedding dress, so the Lord Jesus anticipates the day when we will appear before Him, free from all defilement, clothed in His righteousness, to be His holy bride forever.

And as an engaged woman eagerly, lovingly prepares for her wedding, desirous to be her most beautiful for her groom, so the thought of being wedded to our holy Groom should motivate us to spend our lives here on earth in pursuit of the holiness that we know is our ultimate end and His great desire for His bride.

To be holy is our created purpose. It is our destiny. And it will be the outcome for every true child of God and for the entire body of Christ, according to that wonderful promise in 1 John 3:2—"We know that when he appears *we shall be like him,* because we shall see him as he is."

So what is our response to that certainty? "Everyone who has this hope in him purifies himself, just as he is pure" (1 John 3:3 NIV).

When I consider my created purpose and my ultimate destiny—when I remember that I am a splendid, pure bride-in-the-making—I am inspired to be intentional about pursuing holiness, in anticipation of that glorious day when I will finally be holy through and through.

Do you share His goal for your life? What are you living for? From the time you put your feet on the floor in the morning till you pillow your head at night, are you consciously cooperating with Him and pursuing His eternal purpose to make you holy?

BECAUSE JESUS *DIED* TO DELIVER US FROM SIN

To secure our salvation was no small matter to God. It was (and is) a work of infinite, matchless wonder, sacrifice, and grace. You and I were rebels who spurned God and rejected His right to rule over us. We despised righteousness and cherished our sin. We loved what God hated and hated what He loved. We were sinners—enemies of God and objects of His righteous wrath.

The penalty for our sin was death. Our redemption was costly—it required that a sinless substitute suffer and die in our place. And that is exactly what Jesus did. He took on Himself the full force of the wrath of God, dying in the sinner's place. Why? The Scripture is clear: "Jesus Christ, who gave himself *for our sins* to deliver us from the present evil age" (Galatians 1:3b–4).

In his classic book titled simply *Holiness,* J. C. Ryle writes,

> Surely that man must be in an unhealthy state of soul who can think of all that Jesus suffered, and yet cling to those sins for which that suffering was undergone. It was sin that wove the crown of thorns; it was sin that pierced our Lord's hands and feet and side; it was sin that brought Him to Gethsemane and Calvary, to the cross and to the grave. Cold must our hearts be if we do not hate sin and labour to get rid of it, though we may have to cut off the right hand and pluck out the right eye in doing it.[2]

When we tolerate our sin and refuse to be parted from it, we spurn the love and the grace of Christ; we trample His cross and count His sacrificial death of no value.

Jesus didn't shed His blood so you and I could have a passport to happiness and heaven, while continuing to indulge our lust, anger, and jealousy; our addictions and critical, competitive spirits; our selfishness and pride. His death provides the motivation and the power to say *no* to sin and *yes* to holiness in every area of our lives.

Jesus *died* to make us holy, to deliver us from sin. How, then, can we carelessly or casually continue to sin against such a Savior?

BECAUSE WE ARE SAINTS

We sometimes hear the word *saint* used to describe someone who is unusually pious or virtuous. Some religious traditions venerate particular individuals who have been officially recognized as "saints."

Yet when the apostle Paul wrote to the New Testament churches, he often began by addressing *all* the believers as "saints" (literally, "holy ones" or "set apart ones").

Ironically, many of the people to whom Paul was writing were acting like anything *but* saints. They were guilty of many of the same sins we find among believers today—divisiveness, bitterness, immorality, selfishness, a love affair with the world.

So why did Paul call these early believers "saints"? Because that's what they were! Their sinful hearts had been washed by the blood of Jesus. Paul wanted them to see how incongruous their behavior was with their true nature. He was saying to them (and to us) in effect, "Because you *are* saints, *live* as saints!"

When an unbeliever sins, he is doing what comes

naturally. He sins because it is his nature to sin—he is a sinner. But when a sinner becomes a child of God, he is born anew; he is set apart from Satan and the world to belong wholly to God—he becomes a saint. He is given a new heart, and the Holy Spirit within him begins the process of transforming him into the very likeness of Christ.

> ARE YOU LIVING
> LIKE A SAINT?

As a "new creation" (2 Corinthians 5:17), he desires fundamentally to please God. When he sins, he denies his new identity and acts contrary to the nature into which he is being transformed.

Therefore, Paul tells the Ephesians,

Among you there must not be even a hint of sexual
immorality, or of any kind of impurity, or of greed,
because these are improper for God's holy people [saints].
　　　　　　　　　　　　　　　　—Ephesians 5:3 NIV

Are you a saint? If you are a child of God, the answer is *yes*. You have been chosen and set apart as one of His holy people.

Are you living like a saint? If you are truly a child of God, the answer will be, *Yes—not perfectly, but that is my heart's desire, and by His grace, I am actively pursuing holiness and growing to be more like the One who has saved me.*

Because Our Intimacy
with God Depends on It

Ever since I was born again as a young girl, I have longed to experience a more intimate relationship with God and to enjoy the reality of His presence. The psalmist expressed the same desire when he asked, "Who shall ascend the hill of the Lord? And who shall stand in his holy place?" (Psalm 24:3). His answer ("he who has clean hands and a pure heart"—verse 4) reminds us that only those who have holy hearts and lives can draw near to God.

> ONLY THOSE WHO HAVE HOLY HEARTS AND LIVES CAN DRAW NEAR TO GOD.

"Blessed are the pure in heart," Jesus said, "for they shall see God" (Matthew 5:8). Unholy people cannot fellowship with a holy God. I cannot cling to my impatience, gluttony, slothfulness, and moodiness, and have fellowship with God at the same time.

For what fellowship has righteousness with lawlessness?
And what communion has light with darkness?
—2 Corinthians 6:14 NKJV

A teenager who willfully violates his parents' instructions is going to have a hard time looking them in the eye when he gets home that night. A wife who lies to her husband about why she exceeded their credit card limit is not likely to enjoy marital intimacy when the lights are turned out at night.

So sin destroys our fellowship with God. "For you are not a God who delights in wickedness; evil may not dwell with you" (Psalm 5:4).

We can sing praise choruses loudly enough to be heard in the next county, we can join sell-out crowds in cheering for God at concerts and conferences, we can applaud speakers who stir our emotions, we can have mystical spiritual experiences; but none of that will get us one iota closer to God if we are ignoring or cherishing sin in our hearts.

"Who among us can dwell with the consuming fire?" the prophet asked. "He who walks righteously" (Isaiah 33:14–15). Intimacy with God is reserved for those who are holy: "For the Lord is righteous; he loves righteous deeds; the upright shall behold his face" (Psalm 11:7).

BECAUSE WE ARE GOING
TO LIVE ETERNALLY IN A HOLY CITY

If you were moving to another part of the world, you would give careful thought to how you packed for the move. You wouldn't want to be burdened with snowsuits, mittens, and winter boots if you were planning on spending the rest of your life in a tropical paradise.

Our ministry is in the process of relocating to a brand-new headquarters building. In anticipation of the move, our staff members are in the midst of a massive effort to "sort and eliminate." Unnecessary files, obsolete equipment, worn-out furniture, accent pieces that won't fit with the new décor—anything and everything that won't be needed in the new facility is being disposed of.

The fact is, you and I will soon be moving to our eternal home. How much thought have you given to your ultimate destination and to what you need to do to get ready for the move?

HOW MUCH ATTENTION AND EFFORT ARE YOU DEVOTING TO PREPARING FOR THE MOVE TO YOUR ETERNAL HOME?

Three times in the last two chapters of the Bible, our heavenly home is referred to as "the holy city" (Revelation 21:2, 10; 22:19). The city is holy because it is where our holy God lives and rules. Heaven is a place of indescribable joy and beauty, a place where there will be no sickness or sadness or sorrow. That is because there will be *no sin* in heaven. None. "Nothing unclean will ever enter it" (Revelation 21:27).

How then can we hold on to our sin and think we are ready to go to heaven?

Charles Spurgeon warns,

Dost thou think to go [to heaven] with thine unholiness? God smote an angel down from heaven for sin, and will he let man in with sin in his right hand? God would sooner extinguish heaven than see sin despoil it.[3]

And, as J. C. Ryle points out, those who don't have a heart for holiness can hardly expect to feel comfortable in heaven:

Without holiness on earth we shall never be prepared to enjoy heaven. Heaven is a holy place. The Lord of heaven is a holy Being. The angels are holy creatures. Holiness is written on everything in heaven. . . . How shall we ever be at home and happy in heaven if we die unholy?[4]

In light of the new, holy home God is preparing for us, the apostle Peter says, "Since you are waiting for these, be diligent to be found by him without spot or blemish" (2 Peter 3:14). This world is just a dressing room—a staging area—for eternity. How much attention and effort are you devoting to preparing for the move to your eternal home?

BECAUSE THE WELL-BEING
OF OTHERS DEPENDS ON IT

Robert Murray McCheyne, the nineteenth-century Scottish preacher, said, "The greatest need of my people is my personal holiness." That applies to more than preachers. The greatest need of your mate, your children, your friends, and fellow workers is not your friendship or your acts of service; it is not your abilities or your financial provision; their greatest need is not even your verbal witness of your faith.

> WHAT OTHERS MOST NEED IS TO SEE IN YOU A REFLECTION OF WHAT GOD IS LIKE.

What they most need is to see in you a reflection of what God is like and of the transforming power of the gospel. Your life can create hunger and thirst for God in others' lives and can be a powerful instrument in the hand of the Holy Spirit to draw their hearts to Christ.

On the other hand, your life can cause irreparable damage to others. Adam could not have fathomed how the effects of his sinful choice would reverberate through all of human history: "Many died *through one man's trespass*" (Romans 5:15). So you cannot calculate all the lives that may be turned astray and devastated through what you might consider inconsequential acts of disobedience.

By contrast to Adam's disobedience, the obedience of the Lord Jesus to the will of His Father brought untold blessing to the human race: "*Through one Man's righteous act* the free gift came to all men, resulting in justification of life" (Romans 5:18b NKJV).

Jesus said in His high-priestly prayer, "For their sake I consecrate myself, that they also may be sanctified in truth" (John 17:19).

This verse has often been a source of motivation and challenge to me as I have wrestled with issues of obedience. When I am tempted to secretly indulge my flesh with excessive food or sleep or by watching a video that condones immorality (even if it *is* an old "black-and-white classic"), to be slack in my work, to be harsh with my words, or to yield to self-centered emotions, it helps me to stop and think about the impact of my life on those who look to me as an example.

It's bad enough for me to make choices that hurt my own relationship with God. How much more serious is it to be the cause of someone else deciding to sin? Not only must I choose the pathway of holiness for God's sake and for my own sake; I must also do it for the sake of others.

Other believers are affected by our choices. And,

to a significant degree, *the lost world* determines its view of God based on the lives of those who profess to know Him. A friend once said to me about another believer, "If I was ever to decide not to be a Christian —and I almost did—it would be because of that man." I wonder how many people have been dissuaded from believing in Christ because of something they have seen or experienced from those of us who bear the name of Christ.

Perhaps far more than you imagine, *your children's* personal and spiritual well-being is affected by your obedience to God.

> *Be careful to obey all these words that I command you, that it may go well with you and with your children after you.*
>
> —Deuteronomy 12:28

Parents seldom realize until it's too late how determinative their example is in the lives of their children. Your children see you being warm and gracious with people at church while being rude or irritable with those in your own home. They see you using a radar detector so you can break the law without getting caught. They hear you call in sick to work when they know you're going shopping with a friend. They hear you use language at home that you'd never use in public. They know how you belittle your mate. And they know the only time they ever see you open your Bible at home is when you're preparing your Sunday school lesson.

They know what your moral standards are—not what you've *told* them your standards are, but what they really are. How? Because they know the kinds of videos you rent and what you laugh at on TV and the kinds of books and magazines you bring into your home.

If those kids grow up loving the world and having no hunger for spiritual things, will that be any great surprise? And will you be prepared to give an account for the way your life influenced their choices? In a very real sense, your heart for holiness—or the lack thereof—is shaping the heart and character of the next generation.

IT IS YOUR CREATED PURPOSE AND YOUR ULTIMATE DESTINY TO BE HOLY.

Do you love your sin so much that you are unwilling to relinquish it for the sake of others? Do you care more about indulging your fleshly appetites than about the eternal well-being of those who are following behind you?

Why care about being holy? Why be willing to say *no* to your flesh and *yes* to God, day in and day out? Because the world desperately needs to see what God is like. Because it is your created purpose and your ultimate destiny to be holy. Because of the price Jesus paid to make you holy. Because you are a saint. Because holy people get to see and know God. Because you're getting ready to move to a place where there is no sin. And because your example may inspire someone who is watching you to choose or reject the pathway of holiness.

NOTES

1. Blaise Pascal, quoted in *New Encyclopedia of Christian Quotations*, compiled by Mark Water (Grand Rapids: Baker, 2000), 477.
2. J. C. Ryle, *Holiness: Its Nature, Hindrances, Difficulties, and Roots* (Welwyn, Hertfordshire, England: Evangelical Press, 1985 rept.), 40.
3. *Spurgeon's Expository Encyclopedia: Sermons by Charles H. Spurgeon: "Holiness Demanded"* (Grand Rapids: Baker, 1978), vol. VIII, 465.
4. Ryle, *Holiness*, 42.

THE ENEMY OF HOLINESS

*Gonna get the Good Lord
     to forgive a little sin
Get the slate cleaned
     so he can dirty it again*

*"God I'm only human,
     got no other reason . . ."
Sin for a season . . .*

✳
—STEVE TAYLOR[1]
✳

For more than a dozen summers, Timothy Treadwell, an avid outdoorsman and "bear specialist," lived peacefully and without weapons among Alaskan grizzlies, living alone with and videotaping the bears. He was known for his confident attitude toward the animals, naming them, and often getting close enough to touch them.

In an appearance on the David Letterman show, Treadwell described the bears as mostly harmless "party animals." Two years later, on October 6, 2003, Treadwell and his girlfriend's bodies were discovered after they were fatally mauled in a bear attack in Katmai National Park on the Alaska Peninsula.

The lesson was all too obvious—wild animals

can't be "reformed." Regardless of how comfortable or trusting you may become around them, sooner or later they will act according to their nature. To assume otherwise is to flirt with disaster.

A healthy fear and respect keeps most people from getting cozy with wild beasts. So what makes us think we can get close to a far more deadly beast called *sin*—and survive? Subconsciously perhaps, we tend to think of certain sins as "mostly harmless"—especially if we've played with them for years and never been seriously bitten.

WHAT MAKES ALL SIN SO HEINOUS AND GRIEVOUS IS THAT IT IS *AGAINST GOD.*

I'm reminded of a story a friend told me about a church service he attended recently in which a lay leader stood before the congregation and confessed, "I've become comfortable with a certain level of sin in my life."

This church member hadn't committed adultery or embezzled money from the church. He had simply done what most of us have done—he had become desensitized to the sinfulness of sin and had come to accept its presence in his life in "tolerable" doses.

I believe our perspective on sin will be changed as we take a serious look at its nature and its consequences.

WHAT IS SIN?

If you grew up in the church as I did, you probably learned early on that the essence of sin is breaking God's law. One systematic theology textbook, for example, says: "Sin is any failure to conform to the moral law of God in act, attitude, or nature."[2]

The primary Hebrew word used for "sin" in the Old Testament means "to miss the mark." Other words used to describe sin indicate man's failure to measure up to a divine standard or expectation.

This legal or judicial definition of sin is important and helpful. However, in recent years, I've been struck by the realization that sin is not merely an objective "missing of the mark" or "lack of conformity" to an impersonal standard. Sin is also intensely personal and has profound relational implications. What makes all sin so heinous and grievous is that it is *against God.*

Yes, sin harms others, and yes, there are consequences for those who sin. But above all, sin is against God, for it violates His holy law and character.

Joseph refused to fall prey to the advances of his boss's wife, because he recognized that if he yielded, he would not merely be wronging the woman and her husband; he would not just violate his own conscience and tarnish his own reputation. He was restrained by the knowledge that his sin would be

against God: "How then can I do this great wickedness and sin against God?" (Genesis 39:9). That is
what makes adultery—and every other sin—"great
wickedness."

You and I will never experience appropriate grief
and brokenness over our sin until we come to see
that our sin is against God.

SPIRITUAL ADULTERY

The reason adultery is so devastating to a marriage is that it is a breach of a covenant; it is a violation of a relationship; it rips apart what God has
joined together.

In Scripture, when God wants to communicate
the nature and the seriousness of sin, He often
chooses imagery related to marital unfaithfulness
and sexual sin—strong words like adultery, prostitu-
tion, lewdness, harlotry, and whoredom.

> *You have played the whore with many lovers;*
> *and would you return to me?*
> *declares the Lord. . . .*
>
> *You have polluted the land*
> *with your vile whoredom . . .*
> *yet . . . you refuse to be ashamed.*
> —Jeremiah 3:1–3

Throughout Scripture, God is seen as a faithful, devoted Husband who is intensely jealous for an exclusive relationship with His wife. When His bride is unfaithful, God is pictured as a rejected Lover who has been grievously wronged; He is provoked to righteous anger and grief when a rival lover enters the relationship.

The next time you sin, picture your husband locked in a passionate embrace with a woman he met over the Internet. Think of your father leaving your mother after thirty-five years of marriage and sleeping with a co-worker. Imagine your son-in-law, who you thought loved your daughter, secretly sleeping with prostitutes while away on business trips.

Try to feel the intensity of the shock, the rejection, the pain, the anger that would well up from the innermost part of your being upon discovering the truth.

Then realize that what you would experience would be just a minuscule glimpse of the way God feels about our sin.

Now, imagine your mate walking in the door and saying in a casual tone of voice, "By the way, honey, I've been carrying on a little affair with that gal who works down the hall from me. Nothing serious, really —just a fling. OK, I'll admit we've slept together— but probably not more than six or seven times. I want you to know that I still love you, and I really hope you'll stay with me and keep meeting my needs."

Worse yet, imagine how you would feel if your mate refused to break off the illicit relationship, but continued to sleep with his girlfriend once or twice a week, month after month, year after year, all the while insisting that he really loved you and wanted to keep living with you when he wasn't with her.

How long would it take for you to say, "No! You can't have her and me! You've got to make a choice."

As heartbreaking and revolting as such scenarios are for those who have experienced them, they give us an inkling of what we are doing to our heavenly Husband when we persist in "sleeping" with our sin, while claiming to be committed to our relationship with Him.

Some time ago, I found myself with a deeply distraught friend who had recently learned that her husband had been unfaithful to her. At one point, she collapsed on the floor next to my feet and began to sob uncontrollably. As I knelt beside her and began to weep with her, she said, with deep emotion, "I never imagined I could ever hurt so deeply or feel so rejected!"

For perhaps twenty minutes, this devastated woman just cried and cried and cried, grieving over the breach in the intimate, exclusive relationship she had once shared with her husband. As I held my friend in my arms, I had a whole new sense of what our sin and unfaithfulness does to God. I hope never to forget that picture.

Somehow, the evangelical world has managed to redefine sin; we have come to view it as normal, acceptable behavior —something perhaps to be tamed or controlled, but not to be eradicated and put to death.

> TO SAY YES TO SIN IS TO FALL INTO THE EMBRACE OF A PARAMOUR.

We have sunk to such lows that we can not only sin thoughtlessly, but, astonishingly, we can even laugh at sin and be entertained by it. I have heard virtually every conceivable kind of sin rationalized by professing Christians, including some in full-time Christian service.

I wonder if we could be so cavalier about sin if we had any comprehension of how God views it. Our sin breaks the heart of our Lover-God who created us and redeemed us for Himself. To say yes to sin is to fall into the embrace of a paramour. It is to bring a rival into a sacred love relationship.

WHAT ARE THE EFFECTS OF SIN?

Beyond how sin affects a holy God and how it affects others, it also exacts a price from those who

sin. As surely as the wild animals Timothy Treadwell
had come to trust rose up to attack him, so sin will
make a prey of those who indulge it. *Before* you yield
to temptation the next time, try reminding yourself
of these consequences:

> THE MORE
> GROUND YOU
> CONCEDE TO SIN,
> THE MORE YOU
> DULL YOUR
> CAPACITY FOR
> TRUTH.

Sin will disappoint you. Sin
never pays what it promises.
Without a doubt, sin does yield
pleasure, but—and here's what
we need to remember in the flush
of temptation—those "joys" are
"fleeting pleasures" (Hebrews
11:25).

We've all known what it is to
sinfully indulge our flesh in the hopes of feeling better, finding relief, getting an emotional thrill, or sat-
isfying some inner longing. But do you look back
now and say, "WOW! That was sure worth it!"
Doubtful. If you're honest, you'd probably have to
say, "Whatever gain I derived from that choice was
short-lived. And it sure wasn't worth the price I paid
to get it."

Sinful pleasures just don't last. Once the initial
"rush" wears off, the enjoyment inevitably turns to
emptiness, misery, and shame.

Sin will deceive you. The more ground you con-
cede to sin, the more you dull your capacity for
truth. As your conscience is violated, you gradually

lose your moral compass—your ability to discern right from wrong. You start to think black is white and down is up. You become blind to the seriousness and extent of your sin.

When others try to point out those blind spots, rather than humbling yourself and admitting your fault, you defend yourself or insist you've been misjudged. You begin to think you can get by with sinning, that somehow you can be an exception to the rule, and that you will escape sin's consequences.

Sin will lead you step-by-step through incremental compromises, all the while convincing you that you can handle this, that you're not so bad.

Sin will dominate you. Sin lures us with the illusion that it is the doorway to freedom. The truth is that those who dance with sin ultimately become sin's slaves.

> *The iniquities of the wicked ensnare him,*
> *and he is held fast in the cords of his sin.*
> —Proverbs 5:22

Peter speaks of ungodly, false teachers (masquerading as just the opposite) who entice their hearers to sin: "They promise them freedom, but they themselves are slaves of corruption. *For whatever overcomes a person, to that he is enslaved*" (2 Peter 2:19).

What kind of freedom is it to be under the control of sinful cravings? To feel compelled to yield every time your fleshly appetites demand to be fed? To come running every time the urge to indulge your flesh rings your bell?

Our culture has promoted a "double the pleasure, none of the guilt" sort of lifestyle. And what's the result? We have become a compulsive, highly addicted society. We are *slaves*— slaves to sex, lust, food, entertainment, games, recreation, work, toys, noise, activity, alcohol, drugs, busyness, therapy, and on and on. We have become dominated by the very "pleasures" we thought would liberate us.

> EVERY UNCONFESSED SIN IS A SEED THAT WILL PRODUCE A MULTIPLIED HARVEST.

Sin will destroy you. In October 2003, raging fires devastated massive portions of southern California, consuming more than 750,000 acres, destroying more than 3,600 homes, and claiming twenty-two lives.

Ken Hale, a state Forestry Department division chief, was one of many heroic firefighters who labored tirelessly to control the fires. After being on the fire line for fifty-five hours, Hale spoke of how his perspective changed when he saw the killer-nature of the fires: "As soon as I found out people had died, it changes the entire outlook on the fire. It goes from being an adversary, a worthy adversary, to something that's very deadly, a monster."[3]

Most of us have become so familiar with sin that we no longer see it as a deadly monster. Sin is more dangerous than wild bears, more deadly than blazing forest fires. Ask Nebuchadnezzar, who lost his mind because he refused to deal with his pride. Ask Samson, who was reduced to a pathetic shred of a man because he never got control over the lusts of his flesh. Ask Achan and Ananias and Sapphira, who all lost their lives over "small," secret sins.

It's not just the "serious sins" your neighbor or your co-worker commits that are deadly; your "subtle sins" can be just as destructive. You may never get in bed with someone else's mate; but your heart for God may be just as easily destroyed by allowing the fires of jealousy, anger, self-pity, worry, or gluttony to go unchecked in your life.

J. C. Ryle cautions against being naive about sin's influence, and urges us to see sin for the destructive monster it really is.

> I fear we do not sufficiently realize the extreme subtlety of our soul's disease. We are too apt to forget that temptation to sin will rarely present itself to us in its true colours, saying, "I am your deadly enemy and I want to ruin you for ever in hell." Oh, no! Sin comes to us, like Judas, with a kiss, and like Joab,

with an outstretched hand and flattering words. The forbidden fruit seemed good and desirable to Eve, yet it cast her out of Eden. The walking idly on his palace roof seemed harmless enough to David, yet it ended in adultery and murder. Sin rarely seems sin at its first beginnings. . . . We may give wickedness smooth names, but we cannot alter its nature and character in the sight of God.[4]

Are you content to maintain a "certain level of sin" in your life, as long as you can tame and manage it? Mark it down: *There is no such thing as a small sin.* Every unconfessed sin is a seed that will produce a multiplied harvest. As Charles Spurgeon warned, "Those who tolerate sin in what they think to be little things, will soon indulge it in greater matters."[5]

The moral or spiritual landslides that take us by surprise most often occur because we have paid little or no attention to the cracks and fissures in our walk with God and our moral conduct. Seemingly small, "harmless" compromises snowball and set the stage for tragic consequences.

Sexual sin is the tip of the iceberg that emerges after a host of under-the-surface sins (lust and lying, for example) have been excused or overlooked— both by the guilty party *and,* far too often, by other believers who shy away from confronting sinful practices they observe, for fear of seeming judgmental or intolerant.

I recall a meeting some friends and I had with a man who had been in the throes of an adulterous relationship for some time. As we asked questions and appealed to him to return to God and his family, it became apparent that this man hadn't awakened one morning and decided to devastate his wife and children and lose his job by having an affair. The fact was, for years he had allowed sins such as bitterness, anger, and pride to fester in his spirit. Then, to medicate his "wounded heart," he justified "small" moral compromises, which led to greater compromises and more justification and deceit. Ultimately, he ended up in the vise-like grip of a powerful sexual addiction.

As we listened to him talk, I could hardly believe the toll sin had taken in the life of this man who had once been a faithful, loving husband and dad. He had become hard, bitter, and disoriented—a poster child for the consequences of sin.

He was miserable—sin had not brought him the happiness it promised. His thinking was profoundly twisted and deceived; he was hopelessly trapped (apart from the grace of God, which he was unwilling to appropriate at that point), and he was in the process of self-destructing. Yet he was so attached to his sin that he was willing to live with its consequences rather than reject the sin.

When he initiated the affair, he had no idea where it would lead him. He said, "I figured when I got caught, I'd dump the relationship and go back to my family." Then he said, "What I didn't count on was that I wouldn't be *able* to get out of it." Satan threw out the bait; this man swallowed it, thinking he'd enjoy it for awhile, only to discover that he was ensnared.

As I listened to his story, I found myself thinking, *It's just not worth it! It's not worth it to cling to one single sin. Oh, Lord, please don't let me ever bring reproach to Your name by failing to take sin seriously.*

FACING OUR OWN SINFULNESS

Most people reading a book like this are not in the midst of an affair (though some, no doubt, are playing with fire). But "good" people who have never committed adultery may have a harder time recognizing their own sinfulness. Growing up as I did in the evangelical world, trained to "live right," and immersed in Bible study, church, and Christian friends and activities, one of my greatest personal struggles has been to see myself as a *sinner* and to see *my* sin as truly detestable.

I can attest that when we cease to sense the seriousness of our sin, we also cease to be moved by the wonder of Christ's sacrifice on the cross for sin. Our hearts get dry and crusty—we know that, we've heard that, ho-hum, same-old, so what? We'd never say those words, of course—but truth be told, I know all too well what it's like to hear one more sermon about God's amazing grace, sing one more song about the wondrous cross, go through one more Communion service, sit through one more Passion play—and be strangely unstirred by the whole thing.

As I have worked on this book, the Lord has graciously given me a greater sense of the sinfulness of my sin. I recall one particular evening when I was struck with the image of my sin as spiritual adultery against God; I was overcome with what it cost Him to forgive sins I had committed so casually and hadn't seen to be a "big deal." In the light of His holy presence, sins I had minimized or thought I could "manage" seemed monstrous. I was faced with my depraved heart in a way I had not seen it for far too long.

In that moment, God granted me the gift of brokenness and repentance; I began to sob, feeling myself to be a sinner desperately in need of God's mercy, and crying out to be freshly washed with the blood of Jesus.

As I reflected on that tender time of contrition and confession, I had an overwhelming sense of gratitude and wonder—I could hardly believe that He would be so merciful to *me*. I also had to admit that, though

I could think of occasions when I had wept over the sins of others, I could not remember the last time I had wept over *my* sin.

I'm not suggesting that God intends for His children to live under the weight of sin that has been confessed, or that we should seek gut-wrenching, emotional experiences. But I am convinced that periodically every believer needs to be given a fresh glimpse of the corruption of indwelling sin, apart from which the mercy, the grace, and the cross of Christ cease to be precious in our eyes.

RETURNING AND RESTORATION

The prophet Hosea knew firsthand the rejection of being betrayed by an adulterous mate. His painful experience became an object lesson to show God's people how He viewed their sin. In the final chapter, Hosea pleads with the people to acknowledge their sin and to choose the pathway of repentance:

> *Return, O Israel, to the LORD your God.*
> *Your sins have been your downfall!*
> *Take words with you*
> *and return to the LORD.*
> *Say to him:*
> *"Forgive all our sins*
> *and receive us graciously."*
>
> —Hosea 14:1–2 NIV

Do you need to return to God? Have you become comfortable with "a certain level of sin" in your life? Is God opening your eyes to see the seriousness of your sin before Him? Perhaps you hardly dare to believe that He would receive you. Perhaps you feel you just can't face what you've done.

God's response to His people infuses us with hope. It reveals Him to be a God of amazing, infinite mercy and forgiveness—a Redeemer and Restorer who is willing and able to make all things new for those who truly repent:

> *I will heal their waywardness*
> *and love them freely,*
> *for my anger has turned away from them.*
> *I will be like the dew to Israel;*
> *he will blossom like a lily. . . .*
> *His splendor will be like an olive tree,*
> *his fragrance like a cedar of Lebanon.*
> *Men will dwell again in his shade.*
> *He will flourish like the grain.*
> —Hosea 14:4–7 NIV

Dear friend, believe it, repent, and be restored!

NOTES

1. Steve Taylor, "Sin for a Season." © Birdwing Music/BMG Songs/ C.A. Music. All rights reserved. Used by permission.

2. Wayne Grudem, *Systematic Theology* (Grand Rapids: Zondervan, 1994), 490.

3. Seth Hettena, "Two Huge California Fires Threaten to Merge," Yahoo.com news story, 28 October 2003.

4. J. C. Ryle, *Holiness: Its Nature, Hindrances, Difficulties, and Roots* (Welwyn, Hertfordshire, England: Evangelical Press, 1985 rept.), 7.

5. Charles H. Spurgeon, *1000 Devotional Thoughts* (Grand Rapids: Baker, 1976), nos. 404, 204.

THE FACE
OF HOLINESS

*The more my heart
is taken up with Christ,
the more do I enjoy practical
deliverance from sin's power.*

✷

—H. A. IRONSIDE[1]

✷

If you've been a Christian for any length of time, you have probably struggled with thoughts like those expressed by this discouraged believer:

> I hated myself; I hated my sin. . . . I felt that there was nothing I so much desired in this world [as holiness], nothing I so much needed. But so far from in any measure attaining it, the more I pursued and strove after it, the more it eluded my grasp; till hope itself almost died out. . . .
>
> I cannot tell you how I am buffeted sometimes by temptation. I never knew how bad a heart I had. . . . Often I am tempted to think that one so full of sin cannot be a child of God at all.[2]

Would it surprise you to learn that these anguished words flowed from the pen of one of the most revered heroes in the history of the Christian church?

J. Hudson Taylor, nineteenth-century pioneer missionary to China, was renowned as a man of extraordinary faith, sacrifice, prayer, and devotion. When he wrote these words, Taylor was the leader of a thriving mission enterprise.

For several months, he had carried a burden for greater holiness in the mission and in his own life. He later wrote of that period:

> I prayed, agonised, fasted, strove, made resolutions, read the Word more diligently . . . but all was without effect. Every day, almost every hour, the consciousness of sin oppressed me.[3]

In the fall of 1869, Hudson Taylor found himself at a crisis point. The pressure of circumstances had been building up for months. He had experienced a bout with serious illness, the unbearably hot climate, the stresses associated with overseeing a large and growing ministry, endless demands on his time, and extensive travel under primitive conditions in the interior of China. He found himself with frayed nerves, irritable, prone to harshness, and unable to live the life of holiness he so longed to exhibit.

From his tormented heart, he asked a question you may have asked on occasion, as have I: *"Is there no rescue? Must it be thus to the end—constant conflict and, instead of victory, too often defeat?"*[4]

Still in turmoil, he returned home from a trip to find a letter from a fellow missionary named John McCarthy, who had recently encountered Christ in a new way. His testimony included a quote from a book called *Christ Is All:* "The Lord Jesus received is holiness begun; the Lord Jesus cherished is holiness advancing; the Lord Jesus *counted upon as never absent* would be holiness complete."[5]

> FROM START TO FINISH, THE PATHWAY OF HOLINESS IS A LIFE OF FAITH.

McCarthy went on to describe the radical difference this message was making in his life:

Abiding, not striving nor struggling; looking off unto Him; trusting Him for present power; trusting Him to subdue all inward corruption; resting in the love of an almighty Saviour; . . . this is not new, and yet 'tis *new to me.* I feel as though the first dawning of a glorious day had risen upon me.[6]

As Taylor read McCarthy's letter, he was given a new look at Christ. That look proved to be transformational.

Six weeks later, Taylor received a letter from his sister in England. She poured out her heart about the pressures she was undergoing as a mother with a growing family and the frustration she was experiencing in her own walk with God. In his reply, Taylor eagerly shared with his troubled sister what God had so freshly done in his life:

As I read [McCarthy's letter] I saw it all! . . . I looked to Jesus and saw (and when I saw, oh, how joy flowed!) that He had said, "*I* will never leave *you.*" "Ah, *there* is rest!" I thought. . . .

I saw not only that Jesus would never leave me, but that I was a member of His body, of His flesh and of His bones. . . . Oh, the joy of seeing this truth! . . . It is a wonderful thing to be really one with a risen and exalted Saviour; to be a member of Christ! Think what it involves. Can Christ be rich and I poor? Can your right hand be rich and the left poor? or your head be well fed while your body starves? . . .

All this springs from the believer's oneness with Christ. And since Christ has thus dwelt in my heart by faith, how happy I have been![7]

PRACTICE THE
LOOK THAT TRANSFORMS

From start to finish, the pathway of holiness is a life of faith—faith in the person, the work, and the gospel of Christ. We were justified—declared righteous—by faith in the atoning work of Christ on our behalf. And we are sanctified —progressively made righteous in our practice—not by our own efforts, but through faith in His sanctifying grace.

> AS WE LOOK UPON HIM, WE ARE CHANGED INTO HIS IMAGE.

In looking to Jesus, Hudson Taylor discovered the power to live a holy life. He wrote to his sister, "I am as capable of sinning as ever, but Christ is realised as present as never before. He cannot sin; and He can keep me from sinning."[8]

Jesus can keep you and me from sinning. And when we do sin, it is He who will cleanse and pardon us. Through the cross of Christ, God has made provision for every sin we could possibly commit. His grace is infinitely more powerful than any sinful bondage.

As Charles Spurgeon says so eloquently, such a Savior is a sinner's only hope:

Though you have struggled in vain against your evil habits, though you have wrestled with them sternly, and resolved, and re-resolved, only to be defeated by your giant sins and your terrible passions, there is One who can conquer all your sins for you. There is One who is stronger than Hercules, who can strangle the hydra of your lust, kill the lion of your passions, and cleanse the Augean stable of your evil nature by turning the great rivers of blood and water of his atoning sacrifice right through your soul. He can make and keep you pure within. Oh, look to him![9]

There is something powerful about fixing our eyes on Jesus as we seek to be holy. The apostle Paul put it this way:

> *We all, with unveiled face, beholding the glory of the Lord, are being transformed into the same image from one degree of glory to another. For this comes from the Lord who is the Spirit.*
>
> —2 Corinthians 3:18

As we look upon Him, we are changed into His image. At the moment, our ability to behold the Savior is limited, because we are in these finite bodies and still have to contend with our corrupt flesh. But one day, totally freed from sin, we will be able to see Christ clearly, as He is. Seeing Him, we will adore Him fully and will be drawn to become like Him. In that moment, our transformation into His likeness will be complete.

*Beloved, we are God's children now, and what we will be
has not yet appeared; but we know that when [Christ]
appears we shall be like him, because we shall see him as
he is.*

—1 John 3:2

The longing of my heart—and the longing of every
follower of Christ—is to be like Him. That transformation is not something we can produce on our own,
apart from the power of His indwelling Holy Spirit.
Like Hudson Taylor, you may have been striving and
struggling to be more holy. The Lord Jesus invites you
to cease your striving, to come to Him, and to find
rest for your soul. As you meditate on His magnifi-
cence and follow in His footsteps, He will bring about
in you a marvelous transformation that will be com-
pleted when you finally see Him face-to-face.

KEEP YOUR EYES ON THE PICTURE

I enjoy working on jigsaw puzzles. When I first
open the box, however, it's hard to believe there's
actually a picture in all those odd-shaped pieces. As
I assemble the puzzle, I keep looking at the picture
on the box. It shows me what the puzzle is supposed to look like when it's finished. Without that
picture, I'd be lost.

As we look at the jumbled pieces of our lives,

sometimes it's hard to fathom that they could ever form anything attractive. God has given us a picture that shows what we will look like when He has finished His sanctifying, transforming work in our lives. It's a picture of Jesus. In Christ we see a perfect reflection of our holy God, for "he is the radiance of the glory of God and the exact imprint of his nature" (Hebrews 1:3). He is the pattern for our lives.

We need to be constantly reminded what the finished product is supposed to look like. That's why it's vital that we keep looking at the picture throughout the assembly process.

Jesus is holiness with a face. To be holy is to be like Him. Let's take a closer look at this portrait of holiness in human flesh. As we do, ask yourself how your life compares to Jesus in each of these traits. The answer will help you identify where you are in the process of becoming holy.

Look at Jesus—
Portrait of Holiness

HIS RELATIONSHIP WITH HIS FATHER

* He lived a life of total dependence on His Father. He looked to God to supply His needs, to provide direction for His life and ministry, and to enable Him to fulfill His purpose on earth.

* He was fully surrendered to the will of His Father. He loved the law of God and obeyed it continually.

* He lived to please God rather than men. He was willing to forfeit the approval of men in order to be pleasing to God.

HIS VALUES AND PRIORITIES

* His supreme motivation was to glorify God. He came to earth with no agenda of His own but to fulfill God's purposes and will on the earth.

* He exalted the eternal over the temporal. For example, doing the will of God was more important to Him than eating (John 4:31–34).

HIS RELATIONSHIP WITH OTHERS

* He was selfless and put others ahead of Himself. He had a servant's heart and continually gave of Himself to meet the needs of others.

* He was available to those who needed Him, even when they interrupted Him at inconvenient times—e.g., when He was tired (John 4:6–7), late at night (John 3:2), when

He had planned a "retreat" with His friends (Mark 6:31–34), or during His quiet time (Mark 1:35–39).

❊ He was submissive to human authorities. As a young man He placed Himself under the authority of His mother and Joseph; He taught and practiced respect and submission to civil authorities.

❊ He was merciful and extended forgiveness to those who wronged Him.

HIS WORDS

❊ He spoke only the words His Father told Him to speak. As a result, His words came across with authority and impact.

❊ He always spoke the truth.

❊ He spoke gracious words that ministered to the needs of the hearers.

HIS CHARACTER

❊ He lived a life of praise and thankfulness.

❊ He was bold when people needed to be confronted with wrongdoing; He was courageous when the will of God required Him to do something difficult.

❊ He was not competitive or jealous. He rejoiced when God blessed others or chose to use other instruments (e.g., John the Baptist).

❊ He was filled with the Holy Spirit and manifested the fruit of the Spirit at all times:

▷*Love*. He loved God with all His heart. He loved others selflessly and sacrificially, to the point of being willing to lay down His life for His enemies. He demonstrated all the qualities of love found in 1 Corinthians 13:4–8.

▷*Joy*. He was full of joy in the Lord. His joy was independent of circumstances, because He trusted God's sovereign control in all things.

▷*Peace*. He was calm and peaceful in the midst of storms, in the press of the crowd, and when facing the cross (John 14:27). He had an inner quiet that surpassed human understanding.

▷*Patience*. He was long-suffering; He willingly endured adverse circumstances as well as injuries inflicted by others.

▷*Kindness*. He demonstrated genuine concern for others. He was particularly attentive to people who had been rejected by others. He was thoughtful, considerate, and alert to the needs of others.

▷*Goodness.* His inner moral excellence manifested itself in active good works toward others. "He went about doing good" (Acts 10:38).

▷*Faithfulness.* He was utterly trustworthy and always true to the will of God. He obeyed, served, and loved God faithfully, all the way to the cross.

▷*Meekness.* He endured misunderstanding and abuse without retaliating. He responded meekly to provocation; He was not defensive, but entrusted Himself and His case to God. He was humble—He refused to promote Himself or to seek His own glory.

▷*Self-control.* He was temperate; His natural passions and appetites were always under the control of the Holy Spirit.

The call to holiness is a call to follow Christ. A pursuit of holiness that is not Christ-centered will soon be reduced to moralism, pharisaical self-righteousness, and futile self-effort. Such pseudo-holiness leads to bondage, rather than liberty; it is unattractive to the world and unacceptable to God. Only by fixing our eyes and our hope on Christ can we experience that authentic, warm, inviting holiness that He alone can produce in us.

To be holy is to appropriate His holiness as our own. As Oswald Chambers reminds us,

> The one marvellous secret of a holy life lies not in imitating Jesus, but in letting the perfections of Jesus manifest themselves in my mortal flesh.
> Sanctification is "Christ in you." . . . Sanctification is not drawing from Jesus the power to be holy; it is drawing from Jesus the holiness that was manifested in Him, and He manifests it in me.[10]

No amount of striving or self-effort can make us holy. Only Christ can do that. As we turn our eyes upon Him, we will find Him to be our "priceless treasure, source of purest pleasure."[11] We will begin to desire Him—His beauty, His righteousness—more than we desire the sparkling enticements this world has to offer. And we will be transformed into His likeness.

NOTES

1. H. A. Ironside, *Holiness: The False and the True* (Neptune, N.J.: Loizeaux Brothers, 1980), 33.
2. Dr. and Mrs. Howard Taylor, *Hudson Taylor and the China Inland Mission* (Edinburgh: R & R Clark, 1918), 174, 166–67.

3. Ibid., 174.

4. Ibid.

5. Ibid., 168.

6. Ibid., 169.

7. Ibid., 175–76.

8. Ibid., 177.

9. *Spurgeon at His Best,* compiled by Tom Carter (Grand Rapids: Baker, 1988), 101.

10. Oswald Chambers, *My Utmost for His Highest,* July 23.

11. "Jesus, Priceless Treasure," words by Johann Franck, translated from German into English by Catherine Winkworth.

THE PATHWAY TO HOLINESS:
"PUT OFF"—
SAY "NO" TO CORRUPTION

Be killing sin or
it will be killing you.

❊

—JOHN OWEN[1]

❊

In Patricia St. John's novel *Star of Light,* a British missionary nurse reaches out to an eleven-year-old Moroccan beggar named Hamid. Night after night, she welcomes him and other beggar children into her home for dinner and a warm place by the fire. One evening after dinner, Hamid impulsively steals two eggs from the kind woman's kitchen, just before he and the nurse go out into the cold, rainy night to visit another needy child. The woman takes a torch to light their way on the dark street. However,

To the nurse's surprise Hamid did not wish to walk in the light. He seemed to be taking great care to keep out of the beam, slinking along the gutters, shuffling against the wall. It was very dark and very muddy, and once or twice he slipped a little, clutching his precious eggs tightly in both hands. . . .

He was not enjoying himself at all. He was so afraid of that broad beam of light, and the eggs somehow did not seem worth it. He wished he could get rid of them, and yet at the same time he wanted to hold on to them.[2]

As is so often the case with us, Hamid was torn between his desire to do what was right and his desire to hold onto his sin, even though it was making him miserable.

A letter I received from a disheartened woman illustrates the struggle every Christian experiences at times between fleshly desires and the indwelling Spirit of God.

I've been a Christian for 30 years and am actively involved in my church and Bible study. I keep wondering why my sin nature is the "path of least resistance." A sinful mind-set (worry, anger, doubt) seems to be my "default" mode—unless I'm making an effort, it's where my thoughts seem to go. It seems like as a new creation in Christ, it wouldn't be such a struggle.

I think deep down we'd like to find a pathway to sanctification that is instant and effortless—no long process, no hard battle. The fact is, there is no such thing.

According to Hebrews 12:14, the pathway of holiness requires intensity and intentionality. Various translations help us understand the force of this exhortation.

> *"Make every effort . . . to be holy"* (NIV).
> *"Strive for . . . holiness"* (ESV).
> *"Pursue . . . holiness"* (NKJV).

Or, as Kenneth Wuest translates it: *Constantly be eagerly seeking after . . . holiness.*[3]

In other words, we must make it our constant, conscious ambition and aim to be holy. We have to work at it, concentrate on it, as an athlete sets his sights on winning an Olympic gold medal: He focuses on his objective, he trains and strains to achieve his goal, he sacrifices for it, he endures pain for it, and he puts aside other pursuits for the sake of a higher pursuit.

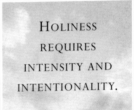

HOLINESS REQUIRES INTENSITY AND INTENTIONALITY.

WEED CONTROL

When it comes to our responsibility in the matter of sanctification, Scripture describes a twofold process that involves "putting off" and "putting on." As children of God in pursuit of holiness, we must "put off" our old, corrupt, sinful way of life and everything that might fuel its growth. And we must consciously "put on" the holy life that is ours through Christ.

These two sides of the coin of holiness often appear within the same passage:

> *Flee* [put off] *youthful passions and pursue* [put on] *righteousness, faith, love, and peace.*
>
> —2 Timothy 2:22

> *Put away* [put off] *all filthiness and rampant wickedness and receive with meekness* [put on] *the implanted word, which is able to save your souls.*
>
> —James 1:21

Another word for "putting off" is *mortification.* It comes from a Latin word that means "to kill" or "to put to death." In a spiritual sense, it relates to how we deal with sin. It indicates that there is a struggle —a battle—involved in dealing with sin and that determined, decisive action is required. It speaks of putting the ax to the root of our sinful inclinations and desires. It implies intolerance for anything in our lives that is contrary to the holiness of God.

Every gardener knows what a constant challenge it is to contend with weeds that keep poking their way through the soil. Those weeds have to be "mortified"—put to death, pulled out by the roots.

Holiness and sin cannot both thrive in our lives. One or the other must die. If we allow weeds of sin to grow up unchecked in our hearts and minds and behavior, the holy life of Christ within us will be choked out.

Mortification involves more than getting rid of things that are inherently sinful. It also suggests the willingness to eliminate influences that may not be sinful in and of themselves, but that could fuel unholy thoughts or behavior and thereby lead us into sin. It means cutting off every possible means to sin.

Some years ago, I discovered that the television had become a weed that was choking out holiness in my life. It was dulling my spiritual sensitivity and diminishing my love and longing for God. Slowly, subtly, the world was stealing my affection, altering my appetites, and seeping into the pores of my being. I found myself being entertained by behavior, speech, attitudes, and philosophies that the world (and many Christians!) would consider acceptable, but that I knew were unholy.

The longer I held on to and justified my viewing habits, the less motivated I was to change. In my heart, I knew that my spiritual life would be better off without the TV. But for many months, though the Spirit was tugging at my heart, I resisted doing anything about it.

One day I finally said, *"Yes, Lord."* I agreed to mortify my flesh—to take decisive action against that which was competing with righteousness in my life. For me, that meant making a commitment not to watch TV anytime I am alone. Almost immediately, my love for God was rekindled, my desire for holiness was renewed, and my spirit began to flourish once again.

WHY ARE WE SO PRONE TO DEFEND CHOICES THAT TAKE US RIGHT TO THE EDGE OF SIN?

It's a decision I've never regretted. On a handful of occasions since, when I have made exceptions to that commitment—for example, to watch news coverage of a major disaster or crisis—I've discovered that it's just too easy for me to drift into making greater allowances and to slip back into old patterns. This is one activity that, for me, needs to stay "mortified" if I am going to keep pursuing holiness!

That approach will sound extreme to some—the word *legalistic* will probably surface in such a discussion. We do need to guard against making absolutes out of personal standards that are not specified in Scripture, or assuming that others are sinning if they don't adopt our standards about issues that may not be traps for them. But why are we so prone to defend choices that take us right to the edge of sin, and so reluctant to make radical choices to protect our hearts and minds from sin?

In the Sermon on the Mount, Jesus exhorted His hearers to be ruthless in cutting off every avenue and enticement to sin.

> *If your right hand causes you to sin, cut it off and throw it away. For it is better that you lose one of your members than that your whole body go into hell.*
> —Matthew 5:30

The apostle Paul put it this way:

> *Put on the Lord Jesus Christ, and* make no provision for the flesh, *to gratify its desires.*
> —Romans 13:14 (emphasis added)

Let me pause and address something I believe is a huge issue among believers today. It's no big surprise to me to see how many professing Christians struggle with lust and sexual sin and "fall" into immoral relationships, when I learn about their entertainment choices—the books and magazines they read, the music they listen to, and the movies they watch.

A woman whose diet includes mostly romance novels or popular women's magazines is setting herself up for moral temptation, if not failure. Anyone who imbibes the sensual culture through movies and other forms of entertainment that feature sexual innuendos, suggestive and immoral scenes, and provocatively dressed women is going to struggle morally—count on it!

I'm going to be blunt here. I have no doubt that I could get drawn into committing emotional, if not physical, adultery, if I do not continually guard my heart. I am not (and never will be) so "spiritual" as to be immune to sexual sin.

Because I want to glorify God and be faithful to Him all the way to the finish line, I have embarked on an intentional pursuit of holiness. I don't want to displease the Lord or bring reproach to His name. Nor do I want to suffer the awful consequences and the destructive effects of immorality. So, as part of my "battle plan," I have resolved not to expose myself to entertainment or other influences that put immorality in a favorable light or could fuel unholy desires.

Further, I have determined, by God's grace, not to allow myself to be in situations where I could be tempted to sin morally—whether emotionally, mentally, or physically. For me, that means no meetings alone behind closed doors with married men and no traveling or meals alone with married men; it means that e-mail exchanges of a personal nature with men get copied to their wives; it means not cultivating personal friendships with married men, apart from the presence and participation of their wives.

Far from being a burden, these "guardrails" have been a huge protection and blessing in my life; they have spared me from many temptations that might easily have drawn my heart away from the Lord.

> ONLY HIS CROSS HAS THE POWER TO STRIKE THE DEATHBLOW TO OUR SINFUL SELVES.

In today's world, such measures seem unrealistic or excessive, even to many Christians. The problem is that most people in today's world aren't in pursuit of holiness; therefore, they think nothing of sin. Behavior that was once considered unacceptable—even by unbelievers —is now considered normal.

But you and I are different—remember, we're *saints!*

That's why we must be serious about *mortifying*— putting to death—our sinful flesh and anything and everything that feeds our flesh.

THE POWER OF THE CROSS

Ultimately, mortification takes us back to the cross. It is at the cross that Jesus died *for* sin and died to sin so we could be free *from* sin. Only His cross has the power to strike the deathblow to our sinful selves. Through reckoning ourselves to have been crucified with Him, our flesh, with its sinful desires, is put to death. According to the apostle Paul, this "death" is a past-tense, accomplished reality for every believer:

Our old self was crucified with him in order that the body of sin might be brought to nothing, so that we would no longer be enslaved to sin. For one who has died has been set free from sin.

—Romans 6:6–7

However, we must also make a daily, determined choice to reject sin's rule in our lives:

Let not sin therefore reign in your mortal bodies, to make you obey their passions.

—Romans 6:12

So how do we live in light of the good news that we are "no longer enslaved to sin"? Use that freedom to say *yes* to righteousness and *no* to sin.

When faced with circumstances or opportunities to indulge your flesh, don't stand around and think about it. Don't fool yourself into thinking you can handle it. Instead, do what Joseph did when Potiphar's wife tried to seduce him: "He would not listen to her."

When she physically threw herself on him one day, he didn't hang around to discuss the situation with her; he acted instantly and decisively—he "fled and got out of the house" (Genesis 39:10–12). He refused to indulge himself, even for a moment, in whatever pleasures an illicit relationship might have offered.

PUTTING THE FLESH TO DEATH

Some of the areas where you need to practice mortification may be different from those for other believers. Overeating (the biblical term is gluttony) has been a lifelong besetting sin for me, and I continually have to mortify my flesh in relation to my physical appetite for food. If you can't control your eating habits, ask a friend or family member to hold you accountable for what you eat and when. Deny your flesh by fasting periodically.

Drunkenness isn't a temptation I struggle with—but if that's an area where you are vulnerable, mortify those desires by staying away from bars; don't allow yourself to hang out with people who drink; cut off every opportunity and occasion to abuse alcohol; purpose to stay away from it. Don't think you can handle "just one drink."

If computer games are constantly calling your name, consuming your time, and causing you to lose your hunger and thirst for righteousness, ask a godly friend to hold you accountable for how much time you spend playing games. Or you may find you need to give them up altogether in order to rekindle your love and desire for God.

If you're being enticed by pornography or lured into unwholesome relationships over the Internet, establish parameters for your computer use that will make it difficult for you to continue sinning. Put your computer in the family room where everyone can see the screen; establish restrictions against using it when you are alone or late at night. If necessary, get rid of your Internet service . . . or your satellite or cable service. Do whatever you have to do to mortify the sinful appetites and lusts of your flesh.

HOW SERIOUS ARE YOU ABOUT WANTING TO BE PURE?

If romantic movies make you discontent with your singleness or dissatisfied with your mate, or if they fuel sexual fantasies in your mind, don't watch them!

If certain magazines or books plant less-than-holy thoughts, desires, or images in your mind, drop your subscription, toss the books.

If you're tempted to become physically intimate with the person you're dating, don't single date. If necessary, take your sister or a friend or your mother with you! If you've already violated biblical standards of purity in the relationship, you probably need to break it off completely. Tough? Yes. The question is, how serious are you about wanting to be pure? If holiness matters to you, you'll be willing to do whatever you have to do to guard your heart and protect yourself—and the other person—from sinning against God.

If you're being drawn into an illegitimate relationship with a co-worker—or a counselor you're seeing (yes, it happens)—get out! Request a transfer, quit your job, cancel your next appointment, find a biblical counselor of the same sex, or ask a married couple to counsel with you. Don't make provision for your flesh!

One woman wrote our ministry and shared that because of her desire to be holy, she actually had to change pediatricians, as she had found herself becoming attracted to her children's doctor and looking forward to appointments so she could be with him.

I'm dead serious about this. And you need to be as well. What did Jesus mean when He said, "If your right hand causes you to sin, cut it off and throw it away" (Matthew 5:30), if He wasn't talking about the willingness to take extreme measures to avoid sinning?

To continue fueling sin or to hold on to anything that is your means to sin is like pouring fertilizer on weeds and then getting frustrated because you can't get rid of the weeds!

Given my battle with gluttony, there are some types of restaurants I have to stay away from, unless I have strong accountability in place, if I want to glorify God in what I eat.

I have a friend who gave up naps because, she said, "they make me sin"! In the past, when she tried to nap, she would inevitably find herself irritated with her children when they disturbed her rest, so she said, "I decided I couldn't take naps, because I was setting myself up to sin."

Now you and I know that restaurants and naps cannot *make* us sin—we *choose* to sin. But I'm talking about being purposeful and intentional in this battle against sin and removing yourself from anything that might fuel your appetite for sin or provide an inducement or occasion to sin. I'm talking about putting away anything that dulls your spiritual sensitivity or your love for holiness.

DEATH BRINGS LIFE

At first hearing, mortification may sound like a difficult, distasteful chore. At times we enjoy our sin too much to want to let it go. We think we'll be miserable if we give it up. But the truth is that those fleshly desires and deeds to which we cling will *keep* us from enjoying the life for which we were created. They will place us in bondage and misery, even as the beggar boy in Patricia St. John's story stumbled miserably down the dark, muddy street, clutching the stolen eggs.

As the story unfolds, Hamid slips and falls in the darkness, badly scraping and bruising his knees and shattering the eggs. When the nurse turns the light of her torch on him, he is covered with mud, blood, and egg yolk. He bursts into tears, terrified at the thought of what she might do, having discovered his theft. Will she call the police or have him beaten or put in jail? He knows he has forfeited the right to her kindness and is certain he will never again be allowed to enjoy the warmth or light of her home.

Instead, to his amazement, the nurse picks him up and takes him back to her home, where she washes him from head to toe, bandages his wounds, and replaces his tattered rags with fresh, clean clothes. She assures him of her forgiveness and explains his need to be forgiven by the Lord and to walk in His light.

> Hamid looked down at his clean clothes and his spotless bandage, and understood. His eggs that had seemed so precious were gone, but he did not want them any more. He had been forgiven and washed

and made clean. He had been brought back into the warmth and shelter of the nurse's home.

They were going out again in the dark to find Abd-el-Khader's house, but it would be quite different now. He would get under the nurse's big, warm coat and walk close beside her, sheltered from the rain; he would not stumble, and he would not be afraid of the light any longer, because he no longer had anything to hide. They would walk guided by its bright, steady beam. It would be a treat.[4]

Not until we mortify—put to death—our sinful flesh can we experience the freedom, forgiveness, and fullness for which our hearts long. Once we have been cleansed and have experienced the joys and satisfaction of His mercy and grace, we will find we no longer want those things we once craved and felt we couldn't live without. To walk in the light with Him will be our greatest treat.

NOTES

1. John Owen, *Of the Mortification of Sin in Believers,* in *The Works of John Owen* (Edinburgh: Banner of Truth Trust, 1995 rept.), 6:9.
2. Patricia St. John, *Star of Light* (Chicago: Moody, 2002), 113–14.
3. Kenneth S. Wuest, *Wuest's Word Studies from the Greek New Testament: For the English Reader,* vol. 2, Hebrews 12:14 (Grand Rapids: Eerdmans, 1973).
4. St. John, *Star of Light,* 116–17.

THE PATHWAY TO HOLINESS:
"PUT ON"—SAY "YES" TO GRACE

Holiness means something more
than the sweeping away
of the old leaves of sin;
it means the life of Jesus
developed in us.

∗

—LILIAS TROTTER[1]

∗

Not long ago, a family in my community began experiencing severe respiratory problems. Investigation led to the discovery that their sickness was being caused by toxic black mold that had spread in their house. Thus ensued a long, arduous process to remove the poisonous substance.

As it turned out, the problem was so pervasive that it could not be solved by a simple cleanup effort; not even a major renovation would suffice. There was only one way to deal with the contamination. They were forced to tear down the entire house —piece by piece, brick by brick—all the way down to the foundation. In its place they erected a completely new, mold-free house.

Virtually all the contents of the original house

had to be destroyed. The owners didn't want to risk bringing any residual mold into the new house.

Sin is a toxin that contaminates to the core of the human soul. When God saved us, it was with the intent of cleansing us from every vestige of sin. He does so through the lifelong process called sanctification. As we have seen, that process—the pursuit of holiness—requires something far more radical than simple reform or renovation. It requires that we put to death—mortify or "put off"—the "old house," that is, the corrupt deeds and desires of our flesh.

However, that's just the beginning. God—the Master Architect and Builder—has drawn up plans to rebuild new, holy lives as we "put on" the Lord Jesus and His righteousness. To put off without putting on is like tearing down a condemned house and thinking your work is complete before the rebuilding is ever begun. Putting off sinful practices isn't sufficient to make us holy. We must also put on righteousness.

> SIN IS A TOXIN THAT CONTAMINATES TO THE CORE OF THE HUMAN SOUL.

For example, in Colossians 3 we are exhorted to "put to death" unholy appetites, attitudes, and actions (e.g., sexual immorality, covetousness, anger, slander, obscene talk, and lying—verses 5–9). The old, contaminated house must be eliminated. In its place, God wants to build a new house as we "put on" the qualities we see in Christ—compassion, kindness, humility, meekness, patience, forgiveness, love, peace, and thankfulness (verses 12–17).

As with putting off sin, putting on the heart of Christ doesn't just happen. We have to be intentional about cultivating new patterns of godliness. This can take place only by the power of the Holy Spirit and the grace of God.

God has provided many different means of grace to help us in the process of putting on holiness. These activities and provisions are not an end in themselves—they are simply means through which we can draw near to God to receive and experience His transforming grace in our lives.

I want to highlight six "means of grace" that have been particularly significant in my personal process of sanctification and spiritual transformation.

THE WORD

The Word of God is one of the most vital agents of sanctification in the life of a believer. Jesus prayed, "Sanctify them by Your truth. Your word is truth" (John 17:17 NKJV).

God's Word has the power to protect us from sin and to purify us when we do sin. David understood the necessity and value of the Scripture in his pursuit of godliness.

How can a young man keep his way pure?
By guarding it according to your word. . . .

I have stored up your word in my heart,
that I might not sin against you.
                                   —Psalm 119:9, 11

As I read Scripture, I often pray that the Lord will wash me with His Word (Ephesians 5:26)—that He will use Scripture to purify my mind, my desires, and my will.

In addition to its cleansing properties, the Word has the power to renew our minds, to transform us into the image of Christ, and to infuse us with Christian graces. When the apostle Paul said farewell to the leaders of the church of Ephesus, he commended them "to God and to *the word of his grace,* which is able to build you up and to give you the inheritance among all those who are sanctified" (Acts 20:32).

YOUR PROGRESS IN HOLINESS WILL NEVER EXCEED YOUR RELATIONSHIP WITH THE WORD OF GOD.

Reading, studying, memorizing, and meditating on Scripture—these disciplines provide weed control and fertilizer for the garden of my heart, guarding and purifying me from sin and stimulating growth in grace.

No believer can withstand the assault of temptation and the encroachment of the world apart from a steady intake of the Word of God. (Nor can we feed on a diet of unholy reading material and entertainment and expect to have pure hearts or to grow spiritually.) Mark it down—your progress in holiness will never exceed your relationship with the Word of God.

CONFESSION

Though we don't hear a lot about this gracious provision in most of our churches, confession—humbly, honestly acknowledging our sin to God and to others—is an essential ingredient for anyone who wants to live a holy life.

We cannot sin and just move on as if nothing had happened, without our spiritual growth being stymied. In fact, Scripture makes it clear that:

> *Whoever conceals his transgressions will not prosper,*
> *but he who confesses and forsakes them will obtain*
> *mercy.*

—Proverbs 28:13

We may not be consciously concealing our sin, but if we do not consciously confess it, we cannot prosper spiritually.

David knew from painful experience what it was like to live under the weight of unconfessed sin—a burden that affected even his physical body and emotional well-being.

> *When I kept silent* [about my sin], *my bones wasted*
>   *away through my groaning all day long.*
> *For day and night your hand was heavy upon me;*
>   *my strength was dried up as by the heat of summer.*
> —Psalm 32:3–4

Not until he was willing to step into the light and uncover his sin did David experience the joy and the freedom of being forgiven and clean once again.

> *I acknowledged my sin to you,*
>   *and I did not cover my iniquity;*
> *I said, "I will confess my transgressions to the Lord,"*
>   *and you forgave the iniquity of my sin.*
> —Psalm 32:5

Many Christians are bowed down under the heavy load of a guilty conscience, with its physical, emotional, mental, and spiritual consequences—all because they do not regularly confess their sin to God.

Biblical confession is first and foremost vertical—toward God. However, it also has a horizontal dimension. When our sin is against others, in addition to confessing our sin to God, we must also acknowledge our wrongdoing and, where possible, make restitution to those we have offended.

Further, confessing our sin to other believers as an expression of humility can be a powerful means of receiving God's grace: "Confess your sins to each other and pray for each other so that you may be healed" (James 5:16 NIV). A couple shared with me recently that one of the key factors in dealing with sinful patterns in their lives has been learning to humble themselves and walk in the light by confessing their spiritual struggles, failures, and needs—not only to God, but to each other.

> CONFESSING OUR SIN TO OTHER BELIEVERS CAN BE A POWERFUL MEANS OF RECEIVING GOD'S GRACE.

What a wonderful provision God has made for us to apply the cleansing blood of Jesus to our defiled consciences and to be sanctified through the act of confession.

COMMUNION

The Lord's Supper is (or ought to be) one of the most vital and sacred practices (hence the name *sacrament,* as it is known by some) in the life of the church and in every believer's life. It is intended to be a time of corporate remembrance and proclamation of the Lord's death, which we are to observe "until he comes" (1 Corinthians 11:26).

Scripture cautions us against partaking of the bread and the cup "in an unworthy manner"; those who do so are "guilty of profaning the body and blood of the Lord" (verse 27). In order to avoid such serious offense, we are warned, "Let a person [first] examine himself" (verse 28). The consequences of failing to do so can be serious, or even fatal: "That is why many of you are weak and ill, and some have died" (verse 30).

I can't help but wonder how many of the physical weaknesses and illnesses experienced by believers are the direct result of God's discipline. Even more sobering is the thought of how many individuals have actually had their lives cut short because their hearts were not pure before God. Only God knows.

The point is that the Communion service should provide a regular opportunity and a powerful incentive for self-examination—making sure our conscience is clear before God and others, and "judging ourselves" so we will not have to come under the chastening hand of God (verses 29–32).

The observance of the Lord's Supper has often been an occasion for needed introspection, confession, and cleansing in my own life. I remember arriving at church one Sunday morning several years ago and realizing that we would be celebrating Communion in the service. As I took my seat, the Lord brought to mind a situation that had taken place months earlier, involving one of the senior members of our church. I had handled a "small issue" in a way that could easily have wounded the spirit of this older man. We had never discussed the matter, but ever since, I had felt awkward whenever I was around him.

As we began to sing the opening songs in the Communion service, I knew that before I could partake of that sacred ordinance, I had to be sure my conscience was clear with that brother. I slipped out of my seat, crossed over to the other side of the sanctuary where he was sitting, and knelt by his side. I expressed my sorrow over what I had done, as well as my desire to be right with him. He graciously forgave me, and I was then free to partake of the Lord's Supper with no known barriers between me and the Lord or any other believer in that place.

THE BODY OF CHRIST

As a woman, knowing my physical limitations, it would be foolish for me to go out walking alone, late at night, in a dangerous part of town. However, it would be an entirely different matter if I were to go out in the company of several strong men who were looking out for me and were prepared to protect me.

As Christians, we have not been left alone to deal with our sin. God has graciously put us into a body of believers who are called to look out for one another and to stand together against the enemies that would threaten our holiness. This family—the body of Christ—is a vital provision God has given to help us in our pursuit of holiness.

This is why it is essential for every believer to be in a committed relationship to a Christ-centered local church. Many believers today think nothing of jumping from one church to another every time they find something not to their liking. In fact, a growing number of Christians don't see the need of plugging into a local church at all. Some are disillusioned with their local church experience. They think they can have an independent relationship with God or that their spiritual needs can be met simply by plugging into the Internet.

Being disconnected from the local church, for whatever reason, is a dangerous way to live. Not only do these "lone rangers" miss out on the blessings of functioning within the context of the body of Christ, but like lone sheep away from the safety of the flock and the watchful care of the shepherd, they are vulnerable to predators of every sort.

Each of us is accountable to God for our personal

holiness. At the same time, God never intended that we should battle sin single-handedly. I frequently ask those in my circle of Christian brothers and sisters for prayer or accountability in areas where I know I am vulnerable to temptation or sin. Is that a sign of weakness? Yes, it is! The fact is, I *am* weak. And so are you. I need the body of Christ. And so do you.

Is it sometimes hard to confess my need and ask for help? Absolutely! It requires that I humble myself and acknowledge that I don't have it all together.

The very pride that keeps you from taking off your mask and getting real is the same pride that will cause you to fall into sin. Humbling yourself by letting others into your life and allowing them to help you and hold you accountable will release the sanctifying, transforming grace of God in your life.

> NO BELIEVER CAN AFFORD TO BE WITHOUT CONSISTENT, DAY IN, DAY OUT ACCOUNTABILITY TO OTHER BELIEVERS.

We also have a responsibility to provide that kind of accountability and help to our Christian brothers and sisters. We cannot stand by on the sidelines when we see fellow believers who are trapped in sinful practices. Scripture requires that we get involved —that we become instruments of grace in their lives, that we actively encourage and help them in the pursuit of holiness.

Brothers, if anyone is caught in any transgression, you who are spiritual should restore him in a spirit of gentleness.
—Galatians 6:1

This kind of mutual encouragement and exhortation must take place on a *daily* basis. Why? Because *it takes less than twenty-four hours* for our hearts to become hardened or deceived by sin (Hebrews 3:13). It can happen to me; it can happen to you. No believer is immune to sin's lure. No believer can afford to be without consistent, day in, day out accountability to other believers.

CHURCH DISCIPLINE

This means of grace is actually a function of "the body of Christ." But Scripture has so much to say about the purifying, restorative effect of addressing sin corporately that it merits being singled out.

Whenever a believer refuses to deal with his sin privately, his sin becomes a public matter that requires the involvement and intervention of others in the body.

One of the fullest treatments of this subject in the New Testament is found in 1 Corinthians 5, where

Paul instructed the church on how to deal with one of its members who had committed immorality and was unrepentant. In a public setting, the church was to totally cut off all fellowship and normal social interaction with this man and to "deliver [him] to Satan for the destruction of the flesh" (verse 5).

By being excluded from the fellowship of believers, the man was symbolically removed from God's protection and was left vulnerable to Satan, who could actually destroy his physical life.

The apostle Paul explained that such extreme measures were for the good of the man himself ("that his spirit may be saved in the day of the Lord"—verse 5). Further, they were absolutely necessary to keep impurity from spreading like gangrene throughout the church: "Do you not know that a little leaven leavens the whole lump?" (verse 6).

This passage describes the most extreme step of church discipline, which is to be taken only after all other routes have been exhausted and rejected. Matthew 18 provides further explanation of that process, in which the offender is repeatedly urged and given opportunity to repent. Seen from this perspective, church discipline is "a severe mercy." It is a gracious provision—not only for the offender, but also for the body.

I attended a church recently that was exercising the final stages of church discipline with two members of the congregation. As the situation was addressed from the pulpit that Sunday, I was reminded of the seriousness and the consequences of sin. I experienced a fresh sense of the fear of the Lord and a renewed longing for God to guard my heart from sin and make me holy. That church's willingness to exercise biblical discipline on unrepentant members had a sanctifying effect in my life and in that entire congregation.

> OUR HEAVENLY FATHER LOVES US AND DISCIPLINES US IN ORDER TO PURGE US FROM SIN.

The fact that so few churches today practice the process of church discipline has made it possible for immorality and ungodliness to flourish within the four walls of most of our churches. How we need to reinstate this means of grace—for our own sakes, for the sake of fallen believers, and for the purity of the whole body.

SUFFERING

No one wants to sign up for the school of suffering. But suffering can be a powerful means of growing in holiness. In fact, the pathway to holiness always involves suffering. There are no exceptions, and there are no shortcuts.

When our lives are all roses with no thorns or all sun with no clouds, we tend to become spiritually complacent and careless and to neglect serious self-examination and confession. Affliction has a way of stripping away the stubborn deposits of selfishness, worldliness, and sin that build up in the course of everyday life.

The psalmist experienced this sanctifying effect of suffering in his life:

> *Before I was afflicted I went astray,*
> *but now I keep your word.*
> —Psalm 119:67

Our suffering may be our heavenly Father's loving response to our sin—sometimes called *chastening* (Hebrews 12:5–11). Suffering may also come in the form of *pruning,* as God cuts away unnecessary or unproductive "twigs and branches" in our lives so we can bear more fruit (John 15:2). We may be required to endure pain for the sake of the gospel, or on behalf of others (2 Corinthians 1:6; 4:11–15). Or our sufferings may simply be the unavoidable pain associated with living in a fallen world that awaits final deliverance from the curse of sin (Romans 8:18–23).

Regardless of its cause, affliction is a gracious gift from the hand of our heavenly Father who loves us and disciplines us in order to purge us from sin and sanctify us. "He disciplines us for our good, *that we may share his holiness*" (Hebrews 12:10).

In Peter's first epistle, the Lord Jesus is set forth as an example of enduring suffering with submission and meekness, so we could be delivered from our sin. The fourth chapter begins with an exhortation that sets forth a powerful principle regarding the sanctifying effect of suffering in the life of a believer.

> *Since therefore Christ suffered in the flesh, arm your-selves with the same way of thinking, for* whoever has suffered in the flesh has ceased from sin.
>
> —1 Peter 4:1 (emphasis added)

Peter urges believers to adopt the same submissive attitude Christ demonstrated when the will of God required Him to suffer. As you suffer, he says, you will be freed from the power of sin.

MAKING IT PERSONAL . . .

What are you doing to cultivate a heart for holiness and to put on the character of Christ? The following exercise will help you assess which of the means of grace we have considered in this chapter you are actively using in your pursuit of holiness, and which ones you may be neglecting.

Don't just skim through these questions—set aside some time to respond prayerfully and thoughtfully, perhaps journaling your answers. If you really want to be challenged, discuss your answers with your mate or with one or more close friends of the same sex who can help hold you accountable to be more intentional in pursuing holiness.

1. THE WORD

* Are you getting a steady, sufficient intake of the Word into your life?

* How has the Word protected you from sin in the past month?

* What passage(s) of Scripture have you meditated on in the past week?

* Are you getting more input from worldly sources or from the Word of God?

2. CONFESSION

* When is the last time you consciously confessed your sin to God?

* Have you committed any sins that you have not confessed to God?

✳ Is there anyone you have sinned against to whom you need to confess your offense and whose forgiveness you need to seek?

✳ Is there any sin you need to confess to other believers to humble yourself, and so they can pray for you?

3. COMMUNION

✳ Do you take the Lord's Supper as a matter of routine? Do you adequately realize the seriousness of this ordinance?

✳ Before partaking of the Lord's Supper, do you examine your heart for unconfessed sin?

✳ Have you been partaking of the Lord's Supper "in an unworthy manner"?

4. THE BODY OF CHRIST

✳ Are you a committed, faithful member of a local church?

✳ When is the last time you asked another believer to pray for you regarding a specific sin or temptation in your life?

✳ To whom are you spiritually accountable in matters of personal and moral purity?

❊ Are you consistently receiving exhortation from other believers regarding your spiritual life?

❊ Do you know another believer who is trapped in some sinful pattern and needs to be spiritually restored? What part does God want you to play in that process?

5. CHURCH DISCIPLINE

❊ Are you under the spiritual authority of a local church?

❊ Does the spiritual leadership of your church know that you welcome accountability for your personal holiness? Would they feel the freedom to confront you over any question-able or sinful practices in your life?

❊ Is there any practice in your life which, if your church knew, would be reason for the process of church discipline to be initiated?

❊ Is there another believer whose sin you have justified or covered, rather than being willing to confront the issue or to allow others to confront it as needed?

6. SUFFERING

❋ How has God used suffering as an instrument of sanctification in your life?

❋ Is there any area of suffering that you are resisting rather than embracing?

❋ Is there any area where you may currently be experiencing the chastening hand of God for your sin? How have you responded to God's discipline?

SUMMARY

❋ Name one or two of these six means of grace that you need to be more intentional about using in your pursuit of holiness.

❋ List two or three steps you will take to allow God to use these means more fully in your life.

❋ Share your response with another believer who will encourage you to follow through on your commitment.

NOTE

1. Cited in *Draper's Book of Quotations for the Christian World,* ed. Edythe Draper (Wheaton, Ill.: Tyndale, 1992), nos. 5748, 312.

THE HEART OF HOLINESS

*Our lives must be such that
observers may peep within doors
and may see nothing
for which to blame us.*

*

—C. H. SPURGEON[1]

*

A family I know has been trying to sell their house for more than a year. They lead busy, active lives and currently have six children living at home. Sometimes they'll go for weeks without anyone wanting to see the house. Then all of a sudden, the real estate agent will call and say, "Can we show your house in thirty minutes?" You can imagine the mad dash that ensues to get the house presentable!

In those frantic "crisis" moments, my friends have become adept at transforming a "lived-in" home with normal clutter into a showcase in record time. The mom grins as she explains how she has learned to stash laundry, dirty dishes, and other assorted house-hold items in places that prospective buyers are unlikely to look—like the clothes dryer . . . and the back of the family Suburban in the garage.

By the time the agent arrives, the residents are nowhere to be seen and the house is in tip-top shape—at least that's how it appears. They just hope no one looks too closely!

How would *you* feel if the doorbell rang right now, and you went to the door to discover you had a surprise visit from distant relatives who were planning to stay for a week and were eager to take a tour of your house? Would you have to scramble to avoid embarrassment?

If you're like me, there are probably some closets and drawers you wouldn't want them to open. Unless you've just finished your spring-cleaning, chances are you'd be hoping your guests didn't look closely enough to see the accumulated dust, the sun streaming through streaked windows, or the cobwebs in the corners.

As Christians, we are called to maintain lives that can be "toured" by outsiders at any time, without embarrassment. A commitment to holiness means having a life that is always "ready for company" and open for inspection—a life that can stand up to scrutiny—not just in the obvious things, but in the hidden places where most might not think to look.

MATCHING INSIDE AND OUTSIDE

Most Christians know how to do a quick pick up in their lives, whenever others come around to take a look. They've learned how to keep up a holy appearance. They know how to look and act "clean" when they're at church or want to leave a good impression on a friend.

But here's the real test: What would others discover if they took a closer look at your life? What would they find if they started opening the closets and drawers of your life?

This is one of the primary issues Jesus had with the Pharisees of His day. They were consumed with keeping up appearances, while content to live with and overlook the mess beneath the surface, where it counted most. The problem wasn't with their outward behavior—their lust for human praise made them star performers. But Jesus could see what the people they were trying so hard to impress couldn't see—their hearts. And that's where the trouble was.

> IS WHAT'S ON THE OUTSIDE THE SAME AS WHAT'S ON THE INSIDE?

As Jesus pointed out, it's not that what's on the outside is unimportant. It's that it's meaningless to present a polished, immaculate image while masking the underlying scum. Such hypocrisy evoked a response from the Lord that was far from mild.

> *Woe to you, scribes and Pharisees, hypocrites! For you are like whitewashed tombs, which outwardly appear beautiful, but within are full of dead people's bones and all uncleanness. So you also outwardly appear righteous to others, but within you are full of hypocrisy and lawlessness.*
>
> —Matthew 23:27–28

No wonder no one wants to be known as a "Pharisee" today! However, like the Pharisees, we have an amazing capacity to feel good about ourselves because we don't commit certain kinds of sins, while brushing off as insignificant the interior pollution of our hearts. So we've never committed physical adultery . . . but we entertain lustful thoughts about someone else's mate. We don't commit acts of physical violence . . . but we harbor hatred toward those who have wronged us and mentally assassinate them or emotionally cut them off.

Does Jesus' description of the Pharisees in any way apply to you?

❋ Is there any hypocrisy in your life? Is what's on the outside the same as what's on the inside? Do you appear outwardly to be godly, while inwardly harboring unholy attitudes, thoughts, or values?

❋ Are you as concerned about the inward reality of your life—that which only God can see—as you are about how you appear to others?

❋ If people could see your inner thoughts and desires, would they conclude that you are a holy person?

MAKING IT PERSONAL . . .

The New Testament authors challenge believers to recognize their position in Christ—justified, redeemed, chosen by God, set apart for His purposes. Then we are exhorted to live a life—inside and out—that is consistent with our position.

The rest of this chapter is not designed to be read in the same way as the rest of the book. I'd encourage you to set this portion aside and make it a part of your personal devotional time over the next few days. Take time to look up each of the following passages from Paul's epistles that describes some aspect of what it means to live a holy life. Then prayerfully consider the application questions.

As with the questions in previous chapters, consider recording your responses in a journal. Then get together with one or more other believers to discuss what God has been saying to you about the condition of your heart and your walk before Him.

Put on the new self (Ephesians 4:17–24)

❋ Are you a new creature in Christ
(2 Corinthians 5:17)?

❋ Is your lifestyle obviously different from those who do not know the Lord?

❋ Could it be that you are struggling and striving to be holy, but finding it impossible, because you have never been made right with God through faith in Christ?

❋ Do you have a spiritually sensitive and responsive heart, or has your heart become hard and cold toward God?

❋ Do you have an underlying desire to be holy and to please God in all you do?

Speak the truth (Colossians 3:9–10; Ephesians 4:25)

❋ Are you an honest person? (Be honest!)

❋ Are you deceiving anyone about anything—in your home? In your workplace? In your church?

❦ Are you pretending to be something that you're not, trying to leave a better impression of yourself than is honestly true?

❦ Are you more concerned about what others think of you than about what God knows to be true?

Put away anger (Ephesians 4:31)

❦ Are you holding anger in your heart toward anyone?

❦ Do you have a hot temper? Do you fly off the handle easily?

❦ Are you easily irritated? Prone to impatience?

Don't steal—give! (Ephesians 4:28)

❦ Have you taken things that don't belong to you? Borrowed things you've never returned?

❦ Are you a hard worker, or are you sometimes slothful or undisciplined in your work? Do you give your boss a full day's work for a full day's pay?

❦ Are you honest in completing expense reports? Tax returns? Taking exams and writing papers for school?

❋ Have you stolen the affections of someone else's mate? Have you defrauded someone of the opposite sex by creating expectations you can't righteously fulfill? Have you robbed anyone of his or her sexual purity?

❋ Are you sensitive to the needs of others and quick to respond to those needs in practical ways?

❋ Are you robbing God by spending on yourself money that belongs to Him?

Watch your tongue (Ephesians 4:29; 5:4)

❋ Do you speak words that are true, pure, good, and kind?

❋ Does profanity, unholy talk, or coarse jesting come out of your lips?

❋ Do you gossip? Slander others with your tongue?

❋ Do you tease others in ways that could be hurtful?

❋ Do you have a critical tongue, perhaps under the guise of being helpful?

❋ Do you speak words that are useless or toxic to those who hear them?

❋ Do your words encourage and build others up? Do your words minister grace to those who hear them?

❋ Do you express thankfulness verbally—to God and to others?

Be sensitive to the Spirit (Ephesians 4:30)

❋ Are you sensitive to the things that grieve the Holy Spirit, or can you sin and not be grieved about it?

❋ Is there anything in your heart attitudes or outward behavior that you know is not pleasing to the Lord?

❋ Are you quick to obey the promptings of the Spirit through His Word and in your heart?

❋ Are you quick to respond to the conviction of God's Spirit when you have sinned?

Put on forgiveness and love (Colossians 3:12–13)

❋ Are you holding a grudge or harboring bitterness in your heart toward anyone? Is there anyone who has hurt or wronged you that you have not fully forgiven?

❋ Is your life marked by love?

Let His peace rule (Colossians 3:15)

❖ Does the peace of Christ control your life, or do you often fret and worry about circumstances beyond your control?

❖ Do you trust the sovereign wisdom and love of God to order your steps?

Be filled with His Word (Colossians 3:16–17)

❖ Do you seek to fill your mind and heart with the Word of God?

❖ Do your conversations with other believers center on the Word and the ways of God?

❖ Is the whole of your life lived in the name and for the sake of the Lord Jesus?

❖ Are you a grateful person? Do you frequently express gratitude to God and to others?

Embrace your God-designed role in the home (Colossians 3:18–21)

❖ Are your family relationships ordered according to the plan God has revealed in His Word?

❖ Wives: Are you submitting to the authority and leadership of your husband? Do you show reverence and respect in your attitude toward him and in the way you talk to him and about him to others?

❋ Husbands: Do you love your wife in the self-less, sacrificial way Christ loves His church? Do you treat her gently and kindly?

❋ Sons and daughters: Are you obedient to your parents' authority?

❋ Parents: Are you giving godly direction to your children?

❋ Fathers: Are you leading your children spiritually in a way that encourages and motivates them to follow Christ?

Holiness in the workplace (Colossians 3:22–23; 4:1)

❋ In your workplace (whether in or out of your home), do you labor as unto the Lord?

❋ Are you diligent in your work? Do you do what you're assigned to do?

❋ Why do you do what you do? Do you have a hidden desire for fame, recognition, or human praise? Are you trying to impress your boss and your fellow workers, or are you trying to please the Lord?

❊ Do you deal fairly with your employees?

❊ Do you treat those you serve, and those who serve you, in a way that is consistent with the way God treats you?

Exhibit godly character (Ephesians 5:1)

❊ Is there anything in your life that does not bear a "family resemblance" to God?

❊ Is there any pattern or practice in your life that, if others followed it, would lead them away from God?

❊ Is your conduct blameless and above reproach in every area of your life—not by the world's standards, but by the standard of God's Word and His holiness?

Be morally pure (Ephesians 5:3)

❊ Are you walking in moral purity and freedom? Is your thought life pure?

❊ Do you guard your heart and your eyes from influences that might tempt you to sin morally?

❊ Are you chaste and discreet in your relationships with members of the opposite sex?

❋ Do you secretly fantasize about a relationship with another man's wife or another woman's husband?

❋ What about the things you read and watch and listen to when you are alone—are they pure, are they lovely, are they holy?

❋ Do you have any secret or private moral habits that are impure?

Avoid the darkness (Ephesians 5:8, 11)

❋ Do you have an appetite for activities you know to be sinful?

❋ Do you enjoy talking with others (or even laughing) about shameful things?

❋ Does your life paint a contrast to the darkness of the world around you and draw people to His light?

Walk in the light (Ephesians 5:8–10)

❋ Do you consciously seek to know and to do what will please the Lord?

❋ Is there any area of your life that could not withstand the scrutiny of His holy light? Any area in which you are not walking as a child of light?

❄ Does your lifestyle mark you as a child of God?

NOTE

1. C. H. Spurgeon, *Twelve Sermons on Holiness* (Swengel, Pa.: Reiner Publications, n.d.); "Holiness, the Law of God's House," 71.

THE PASSION
FOR HOLINESS

*Conspicuous holiness ought to be
the mark of the church of God. . . .
Would God that whenever
they speak of you or me
they may have no evil thing
to say of us unless they lie.*

❊

—C. H. SPURGEON[1]

❊

For more than twenty years, the people of Romania suffered under the iron-fisted, Communist rule of Nicolae Ceausescu—one of the most repressive and corrupt dictators of the twentieth century. Christians were especially targeted by the regime and were subjected to intense intimidation and relentless harassment. Evangelical believers were ridiculed and were referred to in derision as "repenters."

In 1969, the government revoked the preaching license of a pastor in Timisoara. After struggling to find work, the pastor finally ended up gluing paper shopping bags to support his family. For four years, as he did this work, he prayed for revival. In 1973, his license was miraculously reinstated and he was assigned to the Second Baptist Church in Oradea.

From the outset, his ministry in Oradea was characterized by an emphasis on prayer. Church members were encouraged to pray for the salvation of their unbelieving friends, relatives, and colleagues.

However, this pastor's burden was not simply for those outside the church. He was convinced that the revival for which he had been longing and praying all these years must begin in the church. He explained to his people that unbelievers weren't the only ones who needed to repent. Unapologetically, he stressed the need for the "repenters" to repent.

Not content to deal in generalities, he was straightforward in pointing out what he viewed as habitual sins among the "repenters"—issues he believed were hindering the church from experiencing true revival.

In our age of moral ambiguity that asserts every person's right to determine what is right for himself, many will struggle with the stance this pastor took in his church.

For example, he confronted his people about stealing from the state. The government had confiscated and collectivized the farms and factories, forcing the people to turn over to the government the fruit of their labors. The people had felt justified in keeping back from their "own" farms and factories a share of what they believed rightly be-longed to them. The pastor preached that this was wrong and led them to take a vow not to "steal" from the government.

Another issue related to the use of alcoholic bev-erages. Oradea is in an area with many vineyards, and drinking was an accepted part of the culture, even among believers. The pastor believed that drinking alcohol led to sin, and he challenged the believers to take a vow of total abstinence.

Many contemporary evangelicals would be uncomfortable categorizing these particular prac-tices as "sin." While there may be room for discus-sion, the point is that the "repenters" repented—they began to take holiness seriously; they turned from everything they believed was displeasing to God.

When they did, God sent revival. After six months of preaching, praying, and repenting, the fruits of the cleansing began to manifest themselves. One of the most obvious results was the conversion of great numbers of unbelievers. Before the revival began, this church of five hundred members had baptized about ten new believers each year. From June to December 1974, the church in Oradea baptized some two hundred fifty new converts! Approxi-mately four hundred new believers were baptized over the following two years—in a country where a public profession of faith in Christ required a readiness to be martyred for Christ.

The revival could not be contained within a single church. It spread throughout the surrounding area, and its impact was experienced in evangelical churches throughout the entire country. The revived believers were infused with courage and began to stand up for what they believed. Many believe that this fire in the hearts of God's people was one of the elements that ultimately led to the overthrow of the Ceausescu regime fifteen years later.

> THE WORLD IS NOT IMPRESSED WITH A RELIGIOUS VERSION OF ITSELF.

In many of our churches, we're knocking ourselves out trying to be "relevant" so we can attract new members. We don't want to appear to be different, extreme, or too spiritual, for fear of turning off unbelievers. By contrast, once the church in Oradea was willing to be different from the world, the very unbelievers who had once ridiculed them were irresistibly drawn to Christ.

We have accommodated to the world rather than calling the world to accommodate to Christ. When will we realize that the world is not impressed with a religious version of itself? Our greatest effectiveness is not to be found in being like the world; it is to be found in being distinct from the world, in being like Jesus.

The absence of revival in evangelicalism today certainly does not reflect a lack of activity and opportunities. We have more Christian concerts, conferences, programs, strategies, media events, books, tapes, magazines, and radio/TV ministries than any generation in history. In fact, we have more prayer gatherings and more events and resources geared toward "spiritual awakening" than ever. But something is missing.

I remember discussing this matter with a ministry leader who observed, "Lots of people are praying, and lots of people are repenting, but so few are changing their lifestyle." A light went on in my mind when I heard that statement. The fact is, *if people are not changing their lifestyle, they're not repenting.* And if we're not repenting, then all our singing and praising and praying and producing are useless—perhaps worse than useless, because all the noise and activity may deceive us into thinking that we're OK and that we are actually experiencing revival.

TAKING HOLINESS SERIOUSLY

How important is holiness to you? How much thought, attention, and effort do you devote to the pursuit of holiness? Are you intentional about putting away everything that is displeasing to God and living a holy life? Is it your priority—your mission—to be holy?

How important is your children's holiness to you? Do you care more about their grade point average, their batting average, and their earning capacity, or about their purity of heart and life? Are you consciously training them to be godly? Does their sin drive you to your knees? Does it cause you to plead with God to give your children a heart for righteousness and to plead with them to repent?

How concerned are you about the holiness of the body of Christ? Does it grieve you:

- ❋ when Christians are unloving and unforgiving,

- ❋ when they are gossips and gluttons,

- ❋ when they have more interest in possessions and pleasure than in spiritual riches and pleasing God,

- ❋ when they dishonor their parents and divorce their mates,

- ❋ when they are self-absorbed and self-promoting,

- ❋ when they are cantankerous and contentious,

❊ when they use profanity and pornography,

❊ when they can sin glibly and without blushing?

What would happen in our day if the "repenters" were to repent? What if believers were to get honest about their sin and serious about pursuing holiness? Might we not once again experience the manifest presence of God in our churches? Might we not see God supernaturally convert multitudes of lost sinners to faith in Christ?

C. H. Spurgeon put it this way: "In proportion as a church is holy, in that proportion will its testimony for Christ be powerful."[2]

Could we honestly say that most of our churches have a powerful testimony for Christ? If not, what does that say about the condition of the church? And how exercised should we be about all this?

SEWAGE IN THE CHURCH?

If plumbing or septic problems caused raw sewage to overflow into the hallways and aisles of your church, one thing is for sure: The problem would not be ignored. Everyone would be horrified. The health hazard would prompt immediate action. Business would not continue as usual. Services would be relocated and crews would work overtime if necessary, until the problem was resolved.

The fact is that something far more serious than raw sewage is running through the lives of countless professing Christians and most of our evangelical churches. And by and large, we are oblivious to the threat.

The floodgates of unholiness—including willful, presumptuous, blatant sin—have opened within the church. Adultery, drunkenness, abuse, profanity, outbursts of temper, divorce, pornography, immodest dress—such sins among professing believers, often members in good standing of respected local churches, are no longer rare exceptions.

And then there are the more "respectable" forms of sewage that are often overlooked and tolerated among believers—things such as overspending, unpaid debts, gluttony, gossip, greed, covetousness, bitterness, pride, critical spirits, backbiting, temporal values, self-centeredness, and broken relationships. Sadly, the church—the place that is intended to showcase the glory and holiness of God—has become a safe place to sin.

> SADLY, THE CHURCH HAS BECOME A SAFE PLACE TO SIN.

A MISSING MESSAGE

Why are we experiencing such an epidemic of open—and not-so-open—sin in the church today? High on the list of reasons would have to be the fact that for more than a generation, the evangelical church, by and large, has abandoned preaching on sin and holiness.

Whenever I have spoken on the subject of holiness in recent years, the resounding response has been, *"Thank you! . . . Why aren't we hearing this message today?"*

We have tiptoed around Old and New Testament passages that proclaim the holiness of God, His hatred of sin, and His wrath and judgment against unrepentant sinners, preferring to consider only references to His mercy, grace, and love.

We have promoted a "gospel" that says it is possible to be a Christian while stubbornly refusing to address practices or behaviors we know are sinful. We have accepted the philosophy that it's OK for Christians to look, think, act, and talk like the world.

We have made it an offense to admonish people about their sin, either privately or, when necessary, publicly. (If only we were as loath to commit sin as we are to confront it!)

Church Marries World

Lest you think I'm overstating the case, let me share several recent illustrations.

I received a letter from a woman expressing deep concern about the lack of a commitment to holiness on the part of so many "believers." She wrote:

> Worldly entertainment and coarse talk are rampant in our churches. Just this week at a women's luncheon, the conversation was about how aggravating it is to go to an R-rated movie and see people bringing their children in with them. I listened for a couple of minutes; then I couldn't keep silent any longer. As graciously as I could, I said, "Ladies, we are Christians! I can't believe we're even talking about attending R-rated movies!"

I know a man who has been involved in the Christian entertainment industry for many years. I was grieved to learn that he has adopted an "alternate" sexual lifestyle. I asked the mutual friend who gave me the report, "Is the [Christian] company where he works aware of this?" The response was hard to fathom: "It probably would not be a concern if they knew."

A friend told me about a Christian dad who, upon learning that his teenage son had been involved in a ring of kids who were drinking and passing around pornography at school, shrugged off the behavior with, "Kids will be kids! Anyway, soft-core porn isn't the same as hard porn."

Some friends lead a weekly Bible study for kids in their daughter's Christian high school. These students would be considered "the cream of the cream"—some of their parents are on the staff of a large parachurch ministry. Recently, my friends distributed a set of lyrics to several popular songs and asked the kids to discuss whether they agreed or disagreed with the message of each song and the behavior it advocated. Three of the songs had lyrics that were blatantly offensive—for example, a song by rap star Eminem who sings in graphic terms about murdering his mother, accompanied by an endless stream of profanity.

> HAVE WE BEEN LULLED TO SLEEP BY A WATERED-DOWN, COMPROMISED VERSION OF "CHRISTIANITY"?

After analyzing the words, the kids were asked if they would continue to listen to a song even if they disagreed with its message. With two exceptions, the consensus of those teens was yes, they would continue to listen to music with these kinds of degrading messages.

Knowing I was working on this book, my

friends wrote to me about their experience. They
concluded:

> Our hearts are breaking. This is one lost generation.
> We adults and the church have failed to pass the
> baton of holiness on to the next generation. Frankly,
> we don't blame these teens. How can they aspire to a
> life of holiness when they haven't been presented
> with a standard of holiness in the home or from the
> pulpit?

Speaking of which . . . a friend told me recently
about a Christian woman she knows who was elated
that her daughter had just been hired as a salesclerk
at Abercrombie & Fitch, a clothing manufacturer
that is defiant in its blatant promotion of immorality and has been widely boycotted for sexual ex-
ploitation of children in its catalogs. My friend continued, "When most of the Christians you know
(many of whom also happen to be leading Bible
studies) are forever following the latest fad or talking about the latest movie they've just been to see,
you can start to feel like you're from a different
planet!"

As I was writing this chapter, I received an e-mail
from a friend who had just been listening to an influ-
ential Christian radio station in one of the nation's
largest markets. In the past ninety minutes, my friend

had heard half a dozen commercials from a "really nice sounding divorce attorney" advertising his services. I can understand that the secular media would be comfortable selling advertising to a divorce attorney. But how have we come to the point that a *Christian* media outlet would promote something God says He hates?

I wonder—were the believers who were listening to that station as they drove down the freeway that day disturbed by what they heard? Did they even notice? Have they—have we—been lulled to sleep by a watered-down, compromised version of "Christianity"?

You need to understand that these examples are not rare or exceptional. That would be cause enough for concern. But the reality is that this kind of twisted thinking has become characteristic of a growing number of professing believers and is being widely defended in the evangelical world. I have heard these perspectives expressed over and over again, by individuals in many of the most respected ministries and churches in the country.

We are seeing the fulfillment of Vance Havner's prophetic words spoken decades ago: "The world and the professing church first flirted with each other, then fell in love, and now the wedding is upon us."

A Passion for God's Glory

Nehemiah was one man who refused to get sucked in by the allure of the world. He never got accustomed to sin, even when everyone around him had become desensitized. The law of God was written in his heart. And love for God compelled him to care when that law was disregarded.

Nehemiah was one of the Jewish exiles living in Persia. In 444 B.C., fourteen years after Ezra led a group of exiles back to Jerusalem to rebuild the demolished temple, Nehemiah received word that the walls of the city were still in disrepair. Nehemiah left his comfortable job and made the nine-hundred-mile journey to assist his fellow Jews in the restoration of the city. Amid fierce opposition from the determined trio of Sanballat, Tobiah, and Geshem, the walls were finally rebuilt.

Nehemiah became the governor of Judah and, along with Ezra the priest, turned his attention to rebuilding the spiritual and moral foundations that had eroded in people's hearts. Nehemiah 8–10 tells the story of the great revival that transpired when the people were challenged to repent and return to the Word of God they had neglected for so long.

As part of that revival, the people made a covenant with God. Similar to the vows taken by the Romanian "repenters," the terms of their covenant were specific and dealt with issues where God's people had been violating His commands: The people agreed not to intermarry with the unbelieving nations around them, to refrain from buying and selling on the Sabbath, and to support the needs of the temple and the Levites.

After serving in Jerusalem for twelve years, Nehemiah returned to Persia for some unknown period of time—perhaps a couple years. When he returned to Judah, he was shocked to discover that the people had failed to keep the commitments they had made to the Lord and were flagrantly disobeying His Word. They were conducting commerce on the Sabbath, they had neglected the maintenance and care of the temple, and they had married foreign wives who were not of their faith. Nehemiah was intensely distressed and boldly confronted the people over their backslidden condition.

> A SPIRIT OF TOLERANCE BECAME EXALTED OVER A LOVE FOR TRUTH.

The most egregious offense involved Tobiah the Ammonite, the man who years earlier had done everything he could to oppose the work of God in the rebuilding of the city walls. Over the years, the Jewish people had gradually let down their guard. They had begun to socialize with their former enemy; in turn, that had led to more intimate relationships, including marriage ties between Tobiah's family and the family of Eliashib the priest. Over time, any differences between Tobiah and God's "set apart" people had all but disappeared.

Unbelievably, by the time Nehemiah returned, this sworn enemy of God was actually living *in the temple*. This was in direct violation of God's command that no Ammonite should ever be allowed to set foot in the temple. Yet there Tobiah was, living in a room that had been given to him by the priest.

Undoubtedly, this change of affairs did not take place overnight. More likely, one compromise led to another and another. The priests and the people found ways of justifying their actions. A spirit of tolerance became exalted over a love for truth. *After all, Tobiah has turned out to be a nice man and his family fits in so well here. It doesn't seem right to tell him he can't stay, just because he's not a Jew. We don't want to be legalistic about this!*

So godless Tobiah moved into the temple, while the people carried on with "church"—not the least bit troubled over the state of affairs. But to Nehemiah, who cared deeply about holiness, this was an unthinkable situation. He was furious. And he acted decisively.

He physically hurled Tobiah and all his possessions out of the temple; then he gave orders to purify the desecrated rooms. He denounced the evil situation and called the priests and the people to repent.

Why were these offenses such a big deal to Nehemiah? Why did he feel the need to interfere in others' lives? Why wasn't he content to just obey God and leave others alone? Why? Because Nehemiah was compelled by a passion for the glory of God to be displayed in His people.

That passion is evident throughout the book that bears Nehemiah's name. It is seen in the way he worshiped and in the way he prayed, in the career choices

> GOD SIMPLY WON'T MAKE HIMSELF AT HOME IN AN UNHOLY PLACE.

and the personal sacrifices he made, in his tears as he confessed on behalf of the people of God, and in his tenacity as he confronted the enemies of God.

His love for holiness is seen in his commitment to personal integrity—even in the "little things" (e.g., Nehemiah 5:18). And it is seen in his boldness in dealing with the sins of others.

Nehemiah had seen God's people pay a terrible price for their sins. They had been exiled in the midst of nations that did not worship Jehovah, first in Babylon and then in Persia. Nehemiah also had seen that through repentance and obedience, once they were allowed to return to Jerusalem, the people of God had been richly blessed and had experienced great joy. He could not bear to see them lose those blessings by returning to the very sins that had caused them to end up in captivity.

His heart for holiness put him in a tiny minority, even among his fellow leaders. He didn't seem to notice or care. He wasn't trying to win a popularity contest. All that mattered to him was that the holy name of God had been profaned, and he longed for it to be hallowed once again.

TIME FOR THE "REPENTERS" TO REPENT

The parallels between the story of Nehemiah and the church in our day are striking. Lots of people who call themselves believers are churning out a lot of religious activity, but we have rewritten the law of God and we have prostituted the grace of God, turning it into a license to sin.

The spirit of tolerance has triumphed over the spirit of truth. And now, Tobiah is living in the temple. Lust, greed, materialism, anger, selfishness, pride, sensuality, divorce, deceit, ungodly entertainment, worldly philosophies—little by little, we've let down our guard, cultivated a relationship with these sworn enemies of God, welcomed them into our churches, and given them a home there.

Beyond that, we've worked so hard to make lost and backslidden people feel comfortable in our churches that there is little conviction of sin, little life transformation, and little manifestation of the presence of God, who simply won't make Himself at home in an unholy place.

I'm not suggesting that we try to alienate unbelievers in our churches or that irrelevance is a virtue. I *am* saying that sinners ought to be uncomfortable in the presence of a holy God. And that they will never be truly converted until they have experienced the conviction of God's Spirit.

In the midst of such a state, the question is, *Where are the Nehemiahs of our day?*

Where are the men and women who love God supremely and who fear nothing and no one but God? Where are the saints who live like saints—whose lives are above reproach in every matter— in their homes, their work, their speech, their habits, their attitudes, their finances, and their relationships?

> THE WORLD IS WAITING FOR THE CHURCH TO GET RIGHT WITH GOD.

Where are the believers whose eyes are filled with tears, whose hearts ache when they see an unholy church partying and entertaining herself to death, and whose knees are sore from pleading with God to grant the gift of repentance?

Where are the Christian leaders with the compassion and the courage to call the church to be clean before God? Where are the moms and dads and young people who are willing to deal thoroughly and decisively with everything that is unholy in their hearts and their homes?

The church has been waiting for the world to get right with God. When will we realize that the world is waiting for the church to get right with God?

Oh, child of God, it is time for the "repenters" to repent. We can scarcely imagine the impact that will be felt in our world when we do.

I will vindicate the holiness of my great name, which has been profaned among the nations, and which you have profaned among them. . . . I will sprinkle clean water on you, and you shall be clean from all your uncleannesses. . . . Then they will know that I am the Lord.

—Ezekiel 36:23, 25, 38

NOTES

1. C. H. Spurgeon, *Twelve Sermons on Holiness* (Swengel, Pa.: Reiner Publications, n.d.); "Holiness, the Law of God's House," 70–71.
2. Charles H. Spurgeon, *1000 Devotional Thoughts* (Grand Rapids: Baker, 1976 rept.), nos. 408, 205.

HERE COMES THE BRIDE!

Let us rejoice and exult
and give him the glory,
for the marriage of
the Lamb has come,
and his Bride has
made herself ready.

✦

—JOHN THE APOSTLE[1]

✦

Imagine for a moment . . . we're seated together at a royal wedding. The invitations have been sent, all the preparations have been made, the guests have arrived, the music is playing, the flowers are spectacular—the sanctuary is decked for a king and queen. The bridegroom and his attendants take their places at the front.

The first strains of the wedding march begin to sound. We all rise.

It's hard to see from where we're standing off to the side. Finally, we're able to catch a glimpse of the bride holding the arm of her father as she begins to move down the aisle toward her bridegroom.

We crane our necks trying to take it all in. As she

gets closer, we realize *something is wrong! It can't be—but yes . . . her veil is torn, and it's askew on her head.*

She gets closer, and we see that it's not just her veil—her hair is matted and in disarray. She looks like she just got out of bed. And her face—it's filthy; she has no makeup on.

As she walks by the row where we're standing, we get a closer look at her dress. It's unbelievable. Her gown is disheveled and wrinkled from top to bottom. It looks like it's been stuffed in a drawer for weeks. Not only that—the once-white dress is covered with an awful assortment of dark stains.

Have you ever seen such a sight? *How can this be?*

Then we see the saddest sight of all, as she approaches her bridegroom. It's the look of profound sorrow in his eyes as he realizes that his bride—the one he loves with all his heart—*didn't care enough to get ready for the wedding.*

My friend, there's a Wedding coming.

It's that Wedding toward which all earthly weddings are intended to point us. The bridegroom is a holy Bridegroom, and He must have a holy bride.

And our Savior will have a holy bride. That's why He loved the church and gave Himself up for her. That's why He took all those stains and blots on Himself.

> *. . . to make her holy*
> *. . . and to present her to himself as a radiant church,*
> *without stain or wrinkle or any other blemish,*
> *but holy and blameless.*
>
> —Ephesians 5:26–27 NIV

My goal in life is not that I would be free from problems or pain; it's not that I would be a best-selling author or have a successful radio ministry or get invited to speak at large conferences; it's not that I would have great relationships or be healthy and financially secure.

ARE YOU READY FOR THE WEDDING?

My deepest desire is that I would be a holy woman and that the church of Jesus Christ would be holy.

How I look forward to that day when you and I, along with all the other saints from all ages, walk together down that aisle toward our Beloved Bridegroom. I want to face Him with joy—radiant, unashamed, "dressed in His righteousness alone, faultless to stand before the throne."[2]

Are you ready for the Wedding? If not, what would you have to do to get ready? Is there a sin you need to confess and forsake? Is there a habit you need to give up—or cultivate? Is there a relationship you need to break off—or reconcile? Are there items in your possession you need to get rid of? Are there debts you need to pay? Are there people whose forgiveness you need to seek? Is there restitution you need to make?

Whatever it is, for Jesus' sake, for the world's sake, for His body's sake, for your family's sake, for your sake—*do it*. By His grace and the power of His Holy Spirit—*do it*.

Nothing, nothing, nothing could be more important. Nothing could bring Him greater glory in our world, and nothing could bring you greater joy—both now and throughout all eternity.

Having therefore these promises, dearly beloved,
let us cleanse ourselves from all filthiness of the flesh and
spirit, perfecting holiness in the fear of God.

—2 Corinthians 7:1 KJV

NOTES

1. Revelation 19:7.
2. Edward Mote, "The Solid Rock." Circa 1834; first appeared in Mote's *Hymns of Praise*, 1836.

HOLINESS
Discussion Guide

As You Begin

For most believers, holiness is a concept that evokes mixed emotions and, at best, seems shrouded in mystery. But no word better captures the splendor of who God is and the destination to which He has called us.

The call to pursue holiness is an invitation to experience the blessings and joys of intimacy with God, to be free from the weight and the burden of sin, and to become all He created us to be.

The study of holiness raises many challenging questions and issues. The purpose of this study is not to answer all those questions or solve all those theological dilemmas, but to encourage you to take a fresh look at our holy God and to engage in a lifelong pursuit of the holiness to which He has called us.

GETTING YOUR BEARINGS

When you think you may be lost, one of the first things you try to do is get your bearings—to figure out where you are in relation to where you want to be.

Do you know where you are in relation to the matter of holiness? Here are a few questions to help you find out. Respond as honestly as possible. You'll be asked to revisit these questions at the end of this study, so you can see in what direction you're headed.

1. How important is holiness to you? How much thought, attention, and effort do you devote to the pursuit of holiness? Are you intentional about putting away everything that is displeasing to God and living a holy life?

2. [if applicable] How important is your children's holiness to you? (A good gauge—do you care more about their grade point average, their batting average, and their earning capacity, or about their purity of heart and life?) Does their sin drive you to your knees?

3. How concerned are you about the holiness of the body of Christ? Does it grieve you when you see yourself or others treating sin lightly?

An Important Reminder

Any discussion of holiness necessarily involves the discussion of sin. It's important to remember two helpful boundaries when discussing sin in a group setting:

1. Confess your own sin—not someone else's. No fair confessing your spouse's sin, your children's sin, your best friend's sin—just your own! If someone else sinned against you in a particular situation, you don't need to supply those details and cause someone else in the group to stumble by taking up an offense.

2. Speaking of details, you don't need many to be biblically accurate in your confession. Identify biblical categories of sin that apply to your situation; avoid sharing unnecessary details of the sinful action itself. It's enough for the group to know that you are convicted of gossiping about someone else—without repeating the gossip! Or that you spoke harshly to your spouse—without repeating the insult you uttered to him or her. Too much detail isn't helpful or necessary in most cases.

A good rule to remember is that unless someone has been part of the problem or is being
used by God as part of the solution (e.g., an
accountability partner, a pastor), repeating
the details may just be gossip.

Tips for Group Leaders

Open and close each meeting by praying together.
Ask the Holy Spirit to guide you through the Word,
to help you be real with one another, and to bring
about any needed change in each heart.

Seek to lead by example. You can serve your
group best by modeling a heart for holiness—being
the first to confess your own sin and the first to
encourage others in God's grace at work in them.

Some of the questions in this discussion guide
call for a level of transparency and openness that
many people are not accustomed to. Encourage the
members of your group to respect each other's pri-
vacy by not discussing others' contributions outside of this group. Remind them that God is
patient and gracious with us as He conforms us to
the image of His Son, and that we need to extend
the same patience and grace toward each other.

This discussion guide is designed to be used in
a variety of contexts—from small groups to Sunday
school classes. Feel free to direct the discussion

based on the size of your group and the allotted time. Avoid rabbit trails into secondary or un-related issues. However, don't feel pressured to get through all the questions each time you meet.

Depending on your available time and the size and openness of your group, you may end up only discussing two or three questions.

The goal is to grow together in your under-standing of God and His ways and to experience individually and as a group the reality of the mes-sage of this book.

Keep your group centered on the truth of the gospel: We are *all* sinners in need of a Savior. Help your members steer clear of self-righteous re-sponses to the confessions of others in the group and from condemnation about their own perform-ance by pointing them to the One who is both the author and perfecter of their faith (Hebrews 12:2).

Introduction

Getting Started

What motivated you to read this book and begin this study? What do you hope to get out of it?

Opening Prayer

The Valley of Vision: A Collection of Puritan Prayers and Devotions is rich food for the soul. Read aloud the prayer at the beginning of *Holiness*—either as a group in unison, or have one or more individuals read while others listen. Then discuss this prayer:

- What words or phrases in this prayer describe our natural, sinful condition? What feeling(s) or reaction(s) do those words evoke in you?

- What words or phrases describe God—His character, His grace, and His work on behalf of repentant sinners?

- What words/phrases describe the sinner's appropriate response to this holy, redeeming God?

Going Deeper

1. Review the letter quoted on pages 18 and 19. Briefly discuss the questions that follow: *"[Is this couple] wrong? Are they unnecessarily uptight or narrow-minded? Do these issues really matter? Or are they simply a matter of personal conscience? Do they change with the culture?"* (p. 19).

What Scriptures come to mind that could apply to the issues this couple is wrestling with? (Resist the urge to spend your whole time on this exercise or to end up in a debate about these particular issues! Just share some initial responses and move on.)

2. What have you heard, seen, or experienced recently—in your own life or in others—that highlights the need for holiness among God's people? (Be sure not to reflect negatively on other believers by sharing specific names or private details.)

3. "Holiness and sin both matter—*more than we can imagine. They matter to God, and the more we comprehend their true nature, the more they will matter to us*" (pp. 20–21). Do you think "holiness and sin" matter enough to most believers? If not, why not, and what could increase our sense of their importance?

4. *"I invite you to join me in a radical pursuit of holiness"* (p. 21). What do you think that kind of pursuit might look like? What might be involved in such a pursuit? Do you find this challenge a bit scary? Daunting? Appealing? Why?

5. Discuss the David Brainerd quote at the beginning of the introduction. What could give someone such an intense burden and longing for holiness and for "more of God"? What do you think Brainerd meant by "this pleasing pain"? What does it mean to "press after God"? Have you ever experienced this kind of intense desire in your own heart?

Concluding Prayer

If it expresses the desire of your hearts, one at a time, have each member of the group read aloud the prayer on pages 19–20.

On Your Own

If you've not already done so, take the challenge to pray the prayer on pages 19–20 at least once a day for the next thirty days. Begin to take note of how God is answering this prayer in your life.

Grace Note

Our natural flesh has no appetite for holiness, so don't be discouraged if your honest answers to the questions at the beginning of this study (page 184) reveal that you are not sufficiently concerned about holiness in your life or the lives of those around you—right now. Remember that God gives grace to the humble. You are on a journey, and God won't leave you where you are today.

Chapter One:
THE SPLENDOR OF HOLINESS

Getting Started

"Holiness isn't exactly an easy subject to 'sell'" (p. 25). Do you agree? If so, why do you think that is the case?

Going Deeper

1. Discuss C. S. Lewis' quote at the beginning of the chapter (p. 23). Do you think most unbelievers think of "holiness" as something *dull* or as something *irresistible?* Why? What about most believers? Why?

2. Review the two facets of holiness explained in this chapter (pp. 29–34).

3. In what sense is holiness the fruit of a relationship?

4. What is the resource that gives us the desire and the power to be holy?

5. *"To resist holiness or to be halfhearted about its pursuit is to forfeit true joy"* (p. 39). Do you

agree? How would you explain to someone else the connection between *holiness* and *joy*?

6. This chapter included the account of the elderly couple who moved out of their home and left nothing behind that was inconsistent with their profession of faith (pp. 36–37). Do you think the same thing would be said if someone were to go through "the record of your life"? If not, what would you need to do for that to be true?

7. How do you respond to the concept of "extreme holiness" found in this chapter?

Pray About It

Thank God for His nature and character. Ask Him to give you a new sense of joy and delight in the concept of holiness.

On Your Own

Begin to highlight and make a list of every reference to holiness that you come across in the Scripture (include words like *holy, clean, pure, righteousness, upright,* etc.). Continue to do so throughout the course of this study.

Grace Note

At times our desires for sin feel so strong that

the prospect of pursuing "extreme holiness" may seem burdensome. C. S. Lewis uses a wonderful word picture that helps put things in proper perspective:

> If we consider the unblushing promises of reward and the staggering nature of the rewards promised in the Gospels, it would seem that our Lord finds our desires not too strong but too weak. We are half-hearted creatures fooling about with drink and sex and ambition, when infinite joy is offered us, like an ignorant child who wants to go on making mudpies in a slum because he cannot imagine what is meant by the offer of a holiday at the sea. We are far too easily pleased.

Chapter Two:
THE MOTIVATION
FOR HOLINESS

Getting Started

Name an individual you have known who has "made God believable" to you. What is it about his or her life that has increased your desire to know God and to become more like Him?

Going Deeper

1. "Why care about being holy? *Why be willing to say no to your flesh and yes to God, day in and day out?*" (p. 60). Review the seven biblical motivations for holy living considered in this chapter.

2. Did any of these points raise a thought you had not seriously considered before as a motivation to pursue holiness?

3. Which of these motivations do you find particularly compelling in terms of your personal pursuit of holiness?

4. Holiness is God's stated goal for every believer. What lesser, competing priorities can tend to consume our time, energy, and focus as believers?

5. How does Christ's sacrifice on the cross provide a motivation to pursue holiness?

6. Can you think of an example of an unbeliever whose view of God was negatively affected by something she saw in a so-called Christian? What about an instance in which an unbeliever was drawn to Christ because of what he saw in a believer?

7. Identify as many categories as you can of people who are watching you and who may either choose or reject the pathway of holiness based on the example of your life (e.g., your family, colleagues at work).

8. *"This world is just a dressing room—a staging area for eternity. How much attention and effort are you devoting to preparing for the move to your eternal home?"* (p. 56). What kinds of things could/should you be doing now to get ready for that move?

On Your Own

Continue compiling biblical references to holiness. As you review your list, note which of the passages might fall under one of the seven motivations for holy living.

Grace Note

On the topic of holiness, it can't be repeated too often: While we do bear personal responsibility for our choices, holiness is not anything we can work up in our own strength. It's grace in action. Remember that every small victory in changing your motivations is a reason to vigorously praise God for His divine help!

Chapter Three:
THE ENEMY
OF HOLINESS

Getting Started

This chapter opens with a story of a man who underestimated the true nature of grizzly bears. Have you ever underestimated something extremely dangerous—a storm, an animal, explosives? Share your story and what you learned.

Going Deeper

1. How did this chapter influence your understanding of and your attitude toward sin?

2. *"I wonder if we could be so cavalier about sin if we had any comprehension of how God views it"* (p. 71). How does God view our sin? Why is it important to come to grips with the fact that our sin is a relational offense *against God?* How does the image of spiritual adultery affect your perspective on your sin?

3. *"'I've become comfortable with a certain level of sin in my life'"* (p. 66). Can you relate to that confession? If so, share an example (past or

present) of how you have become desensitized and come to accept sin in your life in "tolerable" doses.

4. *"Beyond how sin affects a holy God and how it affects others, it also exacts a price from those who sin"* (pp. 71–72). Discuss the four consequences of sin considered in this chapter (pp. 72–76). Between the members of your group, see if you can come up with a real-life illustration of each of those consequences.

5. "There is no such thing as a small sin. *Every unconfessed sin is a seed that will produce a multiplied harvest"* (p. 76). Can you think of an illustration of this principle in your own experience?

6. Does your general attitude and response toward your own sin indicate that you take it seriously and that you are grieved by that which grieves God's heart?

7. In this chapter you read the sad story of a man ensnared by the sin of adultery who thought he'd be able to extricate himself, only to discover he couldn't. There may be those in your group or among your relationships who are struggling with some sinful entanglement.

Galatians 6:1–10 is a helpful passage for such situations. According to this passage . . .

- How are we to think of ourselves?

- How are we to help others?

- What principles or insights do you see in verses 6–10 that could be helpful to someone caught in a sinful snare (or to keep someone from falling into a snare)?

Pray About It

Review the J. C. Ryle quote on pages 75–76. Then take time to pray for a clearer view of the enemy of holiness—sin. Ask the Holy Spirit to convict you and others in your group of any sins that have become like "familiar grizzly bears." If time permits, you may want to break down into smaller groups of men and women for confession and prayer, as appropriate.

On Your Own

Page 75 refers to several people who grew accustomed to their sin or treated it lightly— Nebuchadnezzar, Samson, Achan, and Ananias and Sapphira. What did each of these individuals believe sin would "deliver" for him or her and how was he or she deceived?

Grace Note

Some who read this chapter may be tempted to morbid introspection and melancholy. If that is your response, remember this: Yes, sin is the enemy within and the wages of sin is death. But Christ has overcome that enemy. Be sobered by your sin, but *rejoice* in your Savior!

Chapter Four:
THE FACE
OF HOLINESS

Getting Started

What did you learn from the accounts of
Nebuchadnezzar, Samson, Achan, and Ananias and
Sapphira (from chapter 3) about the nature and
consequences of sin?

Going Deeper

1. Have you ever experienced the kind of struggle, sense of defeat, or discouragement over
your sin that Hudson Taylor describes?

2. How would you explain what it was that was
so transformational in Taylor's walk with God?

3. *"A pursuit of holiness that is not Christ-centered
will soon be reduced to moralism, pharisaical self-
righteousness, and futile self-effort. Such pseudo-
holiness leads to bondage, rather than liberty . . ."*
(p. 96). Can you identify with this statement in
your own life?

4. *"No amount of striving or self-effort can make
us holy. Only Christ can do that"* (p. 97). Discuss

the difference between striving or self-effort, and a Christ-centered pursuit of holiness.

5. What does 2 Corinthians 3:18 tell us about the process of being transformed into the likeness of Christ?

6. Spend some time together simply fixing your eyes on Jesus, in one or more of the following ways.

> • Read aloud one or more of the following passages that describes Him (Hebrews 1:1–3; Colossians 1:13–22; Philippians 2:5–11; Revelation 5).

> • Sing some familiar hymns or choruses that exalt Christ.

> • Praise Him for who He is and for His transforming grace and power in the lives of those He has redeemed.

On Your Own

Read several chapters in one of the four gospels this week. Meditate on what "holiness in human flesh" looks like.

Grace Note

Are you frequently aware of how you fall short of the glory of God? Does it disturb you that certain sin patterns in your life require such great vigilance and constant battle? When you're tempted to give up, meditate upon the *only* One who was perfect holiness in human flesh.

As you ponder the gospels, you will see frequent occasions where the disciples failed as we all do, but you will also discover a Savior who walked in perfect obedience and who has died and been raised again so that we may experience the reality of "Christ in [us], the hope of glory"!

Chapter Five:
THE PATHWAY
TO HOLINESS
(*"Put Off"*)

Getting Started

Have you ever wished for a quick and painless path to godliness? Why do you think God didn't design the Christian life to work that way?

Going Deeper

1. Read 2 Peter 1:3–7. What does this passage tell us about *God's* part in our sanctification? What does it tell us about *our* responsibility?

2. The apostle Paul exhorts us to "Put on the Lord Jesus Christ, and make no provision for the flesh, to gratify its desires" (Romans 13:14).

What does it mean to "make provision for the flesh"? What are some ways you have made provision for your flesh at times? What have been the results? What does it mean to "put on the Lord Jesus Christ"? What are some ways we can do that?

3. This chapter introduces the concept of the mortification of sin—the "putting off" of our old, corrupt way of life. Colossians 3:1–17 offers helpful insights into what we are to put off, as well as what we are to put on in its place. Read through this passage together, one paragraph at a time, considering the following questions:

- **Verses 1–3.** What is the theme and significance of this opening paragraph? (Think about the chapter of this book you discussed in the previous lesson.)

- **Verses 5–11.** What are we to "put to death"? Why should these things no longer be a part of the Christian's life?

- **Verses 12–17.** What are we to put on? Why? How do these qualities compare and contrast with the things we are to put off?

- How are Christians described in this passage? How should that description spur us on to pursue holiness?

Giving Thanks

Did you notice the three references to "giving thanks" in Colossians 3:15–17? Why do you think this passage ends with an emphasis on thankfulness? Wrap up your time by offering up prayers (and songs, if you wish!) of thanksgiving for what you have seen in this passage.

On Your Own

"Be killing sin or sin will be killing you" (John Owen, p. 99). Are you consciously committed to waging war against sin in your life? If so, consider these questions:

• Are there any ways you are "making provision" for your flesh? Are you involved in any activities or practices that could increase your appetite for sin? Is there any source of temptation you are holding on to? Are you in any situation that might diminish your resistance to sin? Is there anything that is dulling your spiritual sensitivity or diminishing your love for God and your desire for holiness?

• What are the "guardrails" you need to erect to keep from swerving into sin? Pick an appropriate accountability partner, confess any specific sins you need to "put off" or areas where you have been making provision for your flesh, and share your proposed "guardrails"—then check in with that person on a regular basis to let him or her know how you are doing.

As you "put to death" that which is not pleasing to God, don't forget to also consciously "put on" your new life in Christ! Select one particular virtue from Colossians 3 that you sense a need for in your life; meditate on how that virtue is perfectly manifest in Christ, and ask God to make that quality real in your life by the power of His Holy Spirit.

Grace Note

No doubt we all have long lists of things we need to "put off." Remember that you aren't asked to make these changes on your own. No one wants to see us "put off" sin more than our heavenly Father! He has given us the Holy Spirit to convict us of sin and help us to change by His grace.

Chapter Six:
THE PATHWAY
TO HOLINESS
(*" P u t   O n "*)

Getting Started

If appropriate, share something God showed you or has been doing in your life as you worked through the "On Your Own" section in the last lesson.

Going Deeper

1. *"Sin is a toxin that contaminates to the core of the human soul. When God saved us, it was with the intent of cleansing us from every vestige of sin"* (p. 120). How do these two statements differ from the way many believers actually live?

Last time, we discussed the concepts of "putting off" sin and "putting on" godliness. But sanctification isn't just about replacing one habit with another. It's about developing love for Christ and a taste for holiness and being filled with His Spirit. This chapter highlighted six ways to experience intimacy with God and to be transformed into the likeness of Christ—six "means of grace."

2. Review these "means of grace" by walking through the "Making It Personal" section on pages 134–38. Discuss how each of these areas is essential in our pursuit of holiness.

3. As you highlight these six areas, share with one another any particular points where you have recognized a lack or a need in your own life. Share any specific steps God has put on your heart for being more intentional in taking advantage of these means of grace.

Giving Thanks

It's not often that you hear Christians praise God for the grace found in things such as confession, discipline, or suffering. But they are indeed praiseworthy because of what they produce in our lives! End this meeting by doing just that.

On Your Own

Which of these "means of grace" need intentional development in your life? List two or three steps you will take to allow God to use these means more fully in your life. Share this plan with your accountability partner. (And don't forget to give an update about your "guardrails"!)

Grace Note

Did you look at the "means of grace" and see another "to do" list? It's really not. It's a lavish menu of transforming grace. It's an arsenal of resources for change. Isn't it kind of the Lord to give us so many avenues for pursuing change?

Chapter Seven:
THE HEART
OF HOLINESS

Getting Started

> "A commitment to holiness means having a life that
> is always 'ready for company' and open for inspection
> —a life that can stand up to scrutiny—not just in
> the obvious things, but in the hidden places where
> most might not think to look" (p. 142).

Does that kind of standard motivate you or dis-
courage you? What can help us *want* to live this
way? What can help us be *able* to live this way?

Going Deeper

1. What was it about the Pharisees that evoked
such a strong response from the Lord Jesus?

2. How would you define hypocrisy? Why is it
so abhorrent to God? Did God reveal any
hypocrisy in your own life as you read this
chapter? How did you respond to the questions
on pages 144–45?

3. Take time to discuss how God worked in your heart through the "Making It Personal" section in this chapter (pp. 145–54). Which points did He identify as areas of need in your life? How are you responding to His conviction?

Pray About It

Close your time by praying for one another in the specific areas of need that have been shared. Thank God for the ways His grace and His Spirit are at work in each of your lives.

Grace Note

A list of questions such as those found in this chapter can be overwhelming for some people. Remember God's not asking us to be reformed into a better version of ourselves—He's wanting to *conform* us to the image of perfection in His Son! "He who calls you is faithful; he will surely do it" (1 Thessalonians 5:24)!

Chapter Eight:
THE PASSION
FOR HOLINESS
Epilogue: Here Comes the Bride!

Getting Started

"Conspicuous holiness ought to be the mark of the church of God" (C. H. Spurgeon, p. 155). What are some of the things our churches today are most known for? Do you think "holiness" would be high on the list of most observers?

Going Deeper

1. Review the story of how God sent revival to Romania in the 1970s. What might it look like today if "the repenters" began to repent—if God's people took holiness seriously and turned from everything they knew was not pleasing to Him? What kinds of changes would take place—in individual believers, in Christian homes, in our churches, in our communities, our nation, and our culture?

2. "We have accommodated to the world rather than calling the world to accommodate to Christ" (p. 160). Do you agree with that statement? If

214

so, what evidences do you see of if being true? Why do you think it is so? What should be true instead?

3. What parallels do you see between the Jews in Nehemiah's day and the church in our day? Why do you think we are seeing such an epidemic of sin in the church (i.e., among professing believers) today? What qualities do you see in Nehemiah's life that are needed in believers today?

4. Share the highlights of this study and what fruit you've seen from reading about and discussing holiness. How has your view of God changed? What about your understanding of holiness? Of sin? How have you been growing in "putting off" and "putting on"? What about growing in the means of grace?

5. The epilogue depicted an unimaginable scene in which a bride doesn't care enough about her groom to get ready for the wedding! There's another Wedding coming soon. *"The bridegroom is a holy Bridegroom, and He must have a holy bride"* (p. 180). Are you ready for the Wedding? If not, what would you have to do to be ready? What can you do to encourage others in the Bride to get ready for the Wedding?

Pray About It

Nehemiah was compelled by a passion for the glory of God to be displayed in His people. Among the first things Nehemiah did when he became aware of the trouble in Jerusalem was to fast and pray for the people of Israel. Let us be faithful to do the same for the bride of Christ. Conclude your study by praying together for the church to take holiness seriously and to be ready to meet her Bridegroom as a radiant bride, "holy and without blemish" (Ephesians 5:27).

On Your Own

At the beginning of this study, you were asked to respond to a series of questions. How would you answer those same questions now?

1. How important is holiness to you? How much thought, attention, and effort do you devote to the pursuit of holiness? Are you intentional about putting away everything that is displeasing to God and living a holy life?

2. [if applicable] How important is your children's holiness to you? Does their sin drive you to your knees?

3. How concerned are you about the holiness of the body of Christ? Does it grieve you when you see yourself or others treating sin lightly?

Revive Our Hearts ™

Calling Women to Freedom, Fullness, and Fruitfulness in Christ

Nancy Leigh DeMoss is an author, conference speaker, and the host of *Revive Our Hearts*, a daily radio program for women. She has numerous booklets, audiotapes, and videotapes to promote personal and corporate revival, and to help women cultivate a more intimate relationship with God.

Revive Our Hearts
P.O. Box 2000, Niles, MI 49120
1-800-569-5959 • www.ReviveOurHearts.com

Revive Our Hearts is an outreach of Life Action Ministries.

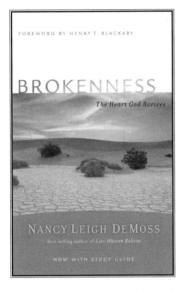

Do you need a fresh infusion of the grace of God in your life? *Brokenness* is an invitation to encounter God in a whole new way. It is a call to discover His heart and His ways; a challenge to embrace a radically new way of thinking and living, in which the way up is down, death brings life, and brokenness is the pathway to wholeness.

Brokenness
ISBN: 0-8024-1281-5

Struggling with stubborn habits? Secret sin? Spiritual strongholds? The key isn't how committed you are to the battle—it's how surrendered you are to God. It is only through a surrendered life that we will receive a host of blessings that cannot be experienced any other way. You can win the battle. You can have the victory. But not until you learn to surrender.

Surrender
ISBN: 0-8024-1280-7

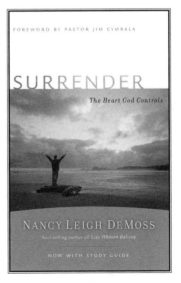

HOLINESS TEAM

ACQUIRING EDITOR
Elsa Mazon

COPY EDITOR
Cheryl Dunlop

BACK COVER COPY
Smartt Guys

COVER DESIGN
Smartt Guys

COVER PHOTO
David Mendelsohn/Masterfile

INTERIOR DESIGN
BlueFrog Design

PRINTING AND BINDING
Versa Press, Inc.

The typeface for the text of this book is
Berkeley